# Beyond Economics

Jan Ott

# Beyond Economics

## Happiness as a Standard in our Personal Life and in Politics

palgrave
macmillan

Jan Ott
World Database of Happiness, Erasmus Happiness
Economics Research Organization
Erasmus University
Rotterdam, The Netherlands

ISBN 978-3-030-56599-2 ISBN 978-3-030-56600-5 (eBook)
https://doi.org/10.1007/978-3-030-56600-5



This Palgrave Macmillan imprint is published by the registered company Springer Nature Switzerland AG.
The registered company address is: Gewerbestrasse 11, 6330 Cham, Switzerland

# Preface

Confusion about the meaning of happiness and well-being can be very frustrating in deliberations and discussions. This is regrettable because happiness and well-being are important and unavoidable subjects in daily conversations and in politics. Happiness is subjective well-being, or well-being as experienced by people themselves. The other type of well-being is objective well-being, or well-being as defined and assessed by experts such as economists, biologists, physicians, and psychologists. If we want to understand well-being, we must pay attention to both types and their mutual relations.

Happiness, as the subjective appreciation of life, is based on the adoption and application of standards. People adopt standards knowingly or unknowingly, and are free to adopt whatever standards they prefer. They may adopt very different standards and even inconsistent or immoral standards, and may change them whenever they want to.

This freedom must be respected, but it can be a source of confusion. Happiness of different individuals will be incomparable if their standards are very different; it will be complicated if they adopt inconsistent standards, and it will be unstable if they change their standards very often. Happiness can even be immoral, and unfit as a general standard, if people adopt immoral standards. Through research we know that people usually adopt consistent, comparable, and morally acceptable standards, and do not change them very often, but there is nevertheless substantial confusion about these issues.

Another potential source of confusion is the relation between overall happiness, cognition, and emotions. It is not unusual to distinguish cognitive and emotional or affective happiness with different dynamics, either as components of overall happiness or as different types of happiness. Both options are acceptable, but we should not define overall happiness as a high frequency of positive emotions and a low frequency of negative emotions. People may value positive and negative emotions in different ways if they apply different standards. Negative emotions can be unpleasant and even painful, but can also be valuable and, perhaps in retrospect, indispensable in someone's life as a whole.

It is therefore respectful to pay attention, first of all, to evaluative happiness, based on some reflection as a cognitive activity. It is also practical since people think a lot about their own life, and they are usually able to answer questions about their evaluative happiness quickly and in a rather reliable way. Attention can then be paid to the different roles of cognition and emotions, and to characteristics like consistency, comparability, stability, and morality. The interaction between cognition and affect is intensive, but it is a good start to assess the results of cognitive evaluation first.

An interesting outcome of happiness research is that it is relatively easy to explain differences in average happiness in nations by an evaluation of actual living conditions, while it is difficult to explain differences in individual happiness. One reason is that more information is needed to explain differences in individual happiness, for example, information about individual genetics, personality, personal experiences, and mental problems. Such information is not readily available in regular statistics and it is difficult to collect such information with simple surveys. Information about actual common man-made living conditions can be found in regular statistics, or collected through surveys. It is fascinating that the dramatic differences in average happiness in nations can be explained quite well. One implication is that differences in collective man-made living conditions play a crucial role for happiness.

Freedom contributes to happiness. There is more of individual freedom and happiness in rich nations thanks to a high level of labor productivity. There are, however, some awkward problems. There are unhappy minorities, for example, relatively poor people and people with mental problems. There is financial insecurity for people with flexible labor contracts, and there is discrimination against minorities. There are high levels of positional competition and commercial manipulation, without proportional benefits. The relations between rich and poor nations are unbalanced. The sustainability of happiness is in danger due to serious ecological developments. Some problems are related to neo-liberalism.

Neo-liberalism is the dominant social-economic ideology in many societies. This ideology has positive consequences for freedom and happiness, but there are shortcomings. The most fundamental shortcoming is arguably that all the needs of the rich are gratified, while the fundamental needs of the poor and their children remain ungratified. A more specific shortcoming is that people are heavily manipulated by commercial advertising. Their individual freedom to decide about standards is undermined. Some other specific shortcomings are unjustifiable inequality, positional competition, financial insecurity, and an upward pressure on production and consumption with negative ecological consequences

It is not the ambition of this book to offer some blueprint for a perfect society, but it does aim to reduce the confusion about the concept and the nature of happiness. Reducing confusion can improve the effectiveness of deliberations and discussions about happiness as subjective well-being and well-being in general. It will make it easier to assess happiness as a potential descriptive standard, or as a potential standard to be pursued, and it will make it easier to identify and analyze the current shortcomings of neo-liberalism.

Reducing confusion can also be beneficial in yet another different way. Many rich people want to change their priorities. They want to put less priority on economic standards like income, and more priority on non-economic standards like happiness. The Corona pandemic supports this development. Many people have to stay home over longer periods. This can be a financial disaster for poor people, but many rich people discover that money is not enough for happiness. A reduction of the confusion about happiness and well-being in general can facilitate this development beyond economics.

Rotterdam, The Netherlands

Jan Ott

# Acknowledgements

On November 27, 2012, I defended my dissertation *An Eye on Happiness; happiness as an additional goal for citizens and governments.* After the approval of the dissertation, I had many discussions with very different people, for example, people with different religious or political convictions and experts with different scientific disciplines. Confusion about happiness and well-being is a recurrent and frustrating problem in such discussions. In this book, I pay more attention to this confusion. Some people who helped me with my dissertation continued their support. Ruut Veenhoven, initiator and Director of the World Database of Happiness, gave valuable advice and the Database was an important source of information. Many volunteers filled this database day by day and bit by bit. Tim Taylor, author of the book, *Knowing what is Good for You: a theory of prudential value and well-being*, helped me again with corrections in linguistics and suggestions in content. And finally: Marian never ceased to encourage me to contribute to a better understanding of happiness and well-being.

# Contents

# About the Author

**Jan Cornelis Ott** studied sociology and law and specialized in social economic policy, labour relations and public administration. He worked as a policy adviser for the Dutch Ministry of Social Affairs and Employment and participated in several Conferences of the International Labour Organization. Since 2004 he has worked as a social researcher at the World Database of Happiness at the Erasmus Happiness Economics Research Organization, at the Erasmus University in Rotterdam. In 2012 he finished his dissertation *An Eye on Happiness; happiness as an additional goal for citizens and governments.* He published many articles about the importance of the quality of governments for well-being and happiness, for example in *The Journal of Happiness Studies and in Social Indicators Research.*

CHAPTER 1

# Introduction: The Confusion About Happiness

## The Scottish Enlightenment Revisited; Pessimism and Optimism About Happiness as a Common Goal; Confusion as an Obstacle

Happiness was an important subject in the Scottish Enlightenment. In 1725 Francis Hutcheson published his *Inquiry Concerning Moral Good and Evil.*[1] The test or criterion of right action is in his view its tendency to promote the general welfare of mankind. People should try to promote this general welfare, and they should do it in an altruistic manner, disregarding their own interests. He anticipated the utilitarianism of Jeremy Bentham, who published *The Principles of Morals and Legislation* in 1789,[2] not only in principle but even in the use of the phrase *the greatest happiness for the greatest number*. A key point in this philosophy is that the morality of behaviour and decisions depends on their impact on happiness. Hutcheson and Bentham clearly accept happiness, not just as an individual goal but also as a common or collective goal.

Hutcheson was a professor in philosophy in Glasgow and had two students who became famous in their own right: David Hume and Adam Smith. David Hume published his *Enquiry concerning the Principles of Morals* in 1751.[3] In this book he argues that we have to discern questions

[1] Hutcheson, F. (1725). Inquiry concerning Moral Good and Evil.
[2] Bentham, J. (1789). The Principles of Morals and Legislation.
[3] Hume, D. (1751). Enquiry concerning the principles of morals.


J. Ott, *Beyond Economics*,
https://doi.org/10.1007/978-3-030-56600-5_1

about *is* and *ought*; or ontological questions about how things actually are and deontological questions about how things should be.

Adam Smith finished his first version of *The Theory of Moral Sentiments* in 1759 and his last version in 1790.[4] In this book Smith argues that the morality of behaviour can be assessed independently of the consequences. Important virtues are prudence, justice and benevolence. "The man who acts according to the rules of perfect prudence, of strict justice, and of proper benevolence, may be said to be perfectly virtuous."[5] He also writes: "Concern for our own happiness recommends to us the virtue of prudence; concern for that of other people, the virtue of justice and beneficence, of which the one restrains us from hurting, the other prompts us to promote that happiness."[6]

Smith apparently respects happiness as a crucial value or touchstone, but he finds that the possibilities of attention and care are limited. People can take care for their own happiness, the happiness of their family, friends and country, but taking care for universal happiness of all rational and sensible beings is problematic.[7] He, therefore, accepts happiness as an individual goal, but he is sceptical about the possibilities to adopt happiness as a common goal. It is important to notice that this scepticism is practical by nature. In contemporary terminology we may say that Smith is doubtful about empathy, as our capability to understand the position and the feelings of other people. This attitude is supported by current insights that empathy only works if people feel they are 'of the same kind'.[8, 9] It is an inconvenient truth.

It is also interesting to notice that Smith, with this distinction between happiness as a personal or collective goal, pays attention to the problem of 'collective-' or 'social choice': how do we get from individual wants or

[4] Smith, A., Theory of Moral Sentiments. Dover Publications, Inc. Mineola, New York. *First version in 1759, last version in 1790.*

[5] Ibid., page 239, first sentence in 'Section III, Of self-command'.

[6] Ibid., page 263, first sentence of 'Conclusion of the first part'.

[7] Ibid., page 238, in Chapter III, 'Of universal benevolence'. "The administration of the great system of the universe, however, the care of universal happiness of all rational and sensible beings, is the business of God, and not of man. To man is allotted a much humbler department, but one much more suitable to the weakness of his powers, and to the narrowness of his comprehension—the care of his own happiness, of that of his family, his friends, his country".

[8] Boom, P. (2013) Just Babies. The origins of good and evil. Crown Publishers.

[9] Kiley Hamlin, J. et al. 'Not like me = Bad: infants prefer those who harm dissimilar others' Psychological Science, Vol. 24, Issue 4 (2013).

preferences to collective actions and policies. This is obviously a key issue in economics and in political science.[10]

Inspired by Bernard Mandeville's *The Fable of the Bees, Private vices, Public benefits*,[11] Smith published *The Wealth of Nations* in 1776.[12] He concludes that it is acceptable, and positive for the general welfare, that people promote their own private interests. This creates the ***invisible hand*** of free markets, and leads to the best possible outcomes. It is clear that Smith distinguishes general welfare and happiness, and that this distinction is important for him. People can create more utility and general welfare, and this can be a common goal, but they cannot create general happiness.

People may therefore promote their own interests, but Smith clearly rejects selfish behaviour and is very critical about Mandeville, who is less moralistic in this respect.[13] It would be incorrect, however, to suggest that Mandeville would approve, or even accept, unethical behaviour; he just wanted to be open minded[14] about human nature and despised hypocrisy, in particular puritan hypocrisy by the church. Smith repeats his rejection of selfish behaviour very explicitly in his last publication of the *Theory of Moral Sentiments* in 1790, 14 years after the publication of the *Wealth of Nations*.[15]

We may conclude that Smith distinguishes happiness and general economic welfare for practical reasons. He accepted happiness as a fundamental value and an individual goal, but he was pessimistic about happiness as

[10] Condorcet, N. (1785) also paid attention to this issue of collective choice in a rather mathematical way in his essay 'Essay on the Application of Analysis to the Probability of Majority Decisions'.

[11] Mandeville B. (1714–1729). The Fable of the Bees, Private vices, Public benefits.

[12] Smith, A. (1776). The Wealth of Nations.

[13] See Smith, Theory of Moral Sentiments, Part VII, Section II, Chapter IV, Of licentious systems.

[14] Mandeville once said about himself: 'I am a Philopirio', or: 'I am a lover of empirical knowledge'. He was very critical about corruption and nepotism. He had to leave Rotterdam after a conflict with some local administrators, and went to London in 1693 where he worked as a physician. He found that governments should control people and steer them in the right direction, but governments can only do so if they accept and understand the facts.

[15] The very first sentence of 'The Theory of Moral Sentiments' is worth noting in this respect: "How selfish soever man be supposed, there are evidently some principles in his nature, which interest him in the fortune of others, and render their happiness necessary to him, though he derives nothing from it, except the pleasure of seeing it". This statement got some nice empirical support in: Knight, John B. and Gunatilaka, Ramani, Is Happiness Infectious? (February 2017). Scottish Journal of Political Economy, Vol. 64, Issue 1, pp. 1–24, 2017.

a common goal. The happiness of other people has to be respected, but people may pursue their own economic interests without being altruistic.

After the publication of *The Wealth of Nations*, Jeremy Bentham developed his ***utilitarianism*** with happiness as the ultimate guiding principle. This terminology is a bit odd. In his book *The Principles of Morals and Legislation*,[16] Bentham uses the phrase *the principle of utility*, even though he admits that the phrase *the greatest happiness or greatest felicity principle* is more appropriate. In his vision the word *utility* does not so clearly point to the idea of pleasure and pain as the words *happiness and felicity* do. He uses the phrase *the principle of utility*—and *utilitarianism*—nevertheless for shortness.

Nowadays we must distinguish utility and happiness, because the terms can no longer be used as synonyms.[17]

At the end of the eighteenth century there was a lot of attention to happiness as a goal. In 1785 George Washington wrote in a letter: "My first wish ..., is to see the whole world in peace, and the inhabitants of it as one band of brothers, striving who should contribute most to the happiness of mankind."[18] Accepting happiness as a common goal is, however, more complicated than accepting it as an individual goal. In 1796 there was a proposal to adopt an article in the first Dutch constitution, proclaiming that: "People become united in society for the purpose of the undisturbed enjoyment of their natural and equal rights and the promotion of each other's happiness." This proposal was never accepted because of the vagueness and broadness of the concept of happiness.[19] Happiness was only introduced in a legal context in the American Declaration of Independence (1776) and in the first article of the French Declaration of Human Rights (1791). Nowadays some nations acknowledge happiness as a general goal,[20] but so far without substantial consequences in actual policies.

[16] Bentham, J. (1789). The Principles of Morals and Legislation.

[17] See Ott, J.C. (2011). Limited experienced happiness or unlimited expected utility, what about the differences? Journal of happiness Studies, 12 (3) 519–524. (Review of the book Happiness around the world: the paradox of happy peasant and miserable millionaires (2009) by Carol Graham; New York, NY: Oxford University Press.

[18] George Washington, 1785, in a letter to Marquis de la Routerie. Citation can be read high in the Obelisk of the George Washington memorial in Washington, DC.

[19] Buijs, P. The Age of Happiness. Dutch Opinions on Happiness during the Enlightenment, 1658–1835. Dissertation, Utrecht 2007, with a summary in English. The critical attitude of Kant about happiness as a value also played a role here.

[20] There is a lot of attention to happiness and well-being in policy and legislation in the UK. Gross National Happiness is even a primary goal in the Constitution of Bhutan since 2008; and well-being has been given high priority in New Zealand since 2019.

## Continuing Confusion

In retrospect we may say that there has always been confusion about the concept and the nature of happiness, for example about the morality and the altruistic or egocentric character, about the difference between utility and happiness, and about the possibilities to assess, explain and understand happiness. There have been many developments in the interpretation of happiness,[21] and empirical research has produced many results in the last decades. We know more about happiness, but it is still a complicated concept and phenomenon, with some troubling ambiguities.

Some relatively new and underestimated complications are related to the dualism and comparability of happiness, and the value-freedom of happiness research. Happiness is nowadays defined as the enduring appreciation of life-as-a-whole. This happiness is in fact a specific type of subjective well-being, as will be explained later. Happiness, as the appreciation of life as a whole, is dualistic because it depends on two components: the *affective* and *cognitive* component.

The affective component is about emotional well-being or the hedonic level of affect. This component depends on the gratification of general human needs, but also on perceived gaps between how life should be, and how it actually is. People have a language with symbols, and can imagine and describe an invisible world, as they would like to have it, as a utopia. They may also be less ambitious and just imagine the real world, but with some important improvements.

It is important to distinguish between short- and long-term affective happiness. Short-term affective happiness is about emotions and moods. Long-term affective happiness is about more enduring mental and emotional dispositions, such as cheerfulness or pessimism. Such dispositions are related to emotional experiences but also to personality and genetic properties. Mental problems, such as anxiety and depression, may have a negative impact on long-term affective happiness.

It is relatively easy to measure short-term affective happiness with questionnaires. Momentary emotions, and emotions during short periods like a day or a week, can be assessed by asking simple questions. The problem is, however, that there are strong fluctuations in emotions and moods. It

[21] In his book 'Happiness, a history' (2005, Atlantic Monthly Press, New York), Darrin M. McMahon describes the developments in the interpretation of happiness since Socrates.

is difficult to assess average emotions and moods, and underlying trends, over longer periods. The measurement of long-term affective happiness is relatively complicated, and there is no consensus, so far, about some simple questions to be used in questionnaires.

The cognitive component in happiness depends on a more stable appreciation of life. This appreciation is, like any appreciation, based on the adoption and application of standards. Standards can be used in just a descriptive way to describe a situation. Usually they have at least some normative content, even if they are only used in a descriptive way. It is informative, in this context, that there are several equivalents for the term *standard*, like *indicator*, *criterion*, *measure*, *norm*, *demand*, *expectation*, *goal* and *value*. There is always some normative connotation or loading, but in slightly different degrees; going up from *indicator* to *value*. *Standard* and *norm* are somewhere in the middle. If we use the phrase *happiness as a goal* or *happiness as a value*, it would imply that happiness has to be pursued, but if we use the phrase *happiness as a standard*, we may still decide to apply *happiness* only as descriptive standard, or to actually pursue it. It is important to accept, however, that there has to be some minimum appreciation of happiness as a standard, even if happiness is only used as a descriptive standard.

People may adopt and apply standards knowingly, but usually they do so unknowingly. The adoption and application of standards are therefore subject to pressure from the social environment, or even manipulation. Such standards can be relatively simple, like standards about income, wealth, the quality of jobs, cars and houses, social relations, appearance, entertainment and hobbies. But standards can also be more fundamental, for example, if they are related to values, like solidarity, justice, equality, individual freedom and morality. With such standards people can appreciate their life and decide how happy they are, but in a further step they can also decide to use this happiness as a new autonomous standard, to be applied, or even pursued, in their personal life or in politics.

People are free to adopt whatever standards they prefer, and to decide about priorities, but they always have to decide about the priority they want to put on their own short- or long-term affective happiness. Affective happiness, or the hedonic level of affect, is always the most trivial and inescapable standard to be applied in the evaluation of life. Children are primarily occupied with this affective happiness, but as they grow older they may adopt alternative standards, such as being social or good-looking, making money or being successful as a pianist or in chess or sports.

There is an intensive interaction between the affective and cognitive component, but they also have their own dynamics and characteristics. It is not unusual therefore to distinguish affective and cognitive happiness as two different types of happiness. This dualism of happiness poses the question of whether we may discern anything like *overall happiness*, or happiness *in general*, or *encompassing happiness*. Or put differently: there is a definition of 'overall happiness', but is there a corresponding reality? If we have to reject this idea, we can only pay attention to either affective or cognitive happiness. This complication is about the consistency of affective and cognitive happiness; or to be practical: about the differences in levels of affective and cognitive happiness, at specific moments or over longer periods. If such differences are small, we may conclude that there is consistency, but we have to be careful if the differences are substantial.

If we may accept the notion of 'overall happiness', we will have to deal with another complication: can we compare the happiness of different individuals, and can we compare the happiness of the same individuals in different periods of time? These two issues are sometimes denoted as the problems of interpersonal and longitudinal *comparability*.

Comparability is always a somewhat intriguing issue. A helpful distinction is made by John Gerring and Craig Thomas between descriptive and causal comparability.[22] Observations are comparable in a descriptive way if they are scorable on some scale, and if the measured attribute, such as self-reported happiness, means the same thing across different contexts. Observations are comparable in a causal way if a cause X has the same relationship with all observations or scores of the dependent factor Y, such as the self-reported happiness of different individuals. Descriptive comparability is a condition for causal comparability.

Put differently: we may say that happiness is always comparable in a descriptive or quantitative way, because we can always compare the appreciation of life of different people, if this appreciation is expressed in scores on some numerical scale, like a 1 to 10 scale. But if this appreciation is based on very different standards, then the meaning and the determinants of self-reported happiness will be different as well. Then we cannot compare happiness in a more qualitative causal way and we are not able to explain differences in happiness. We can turn this argument around: if we

[22] Gerring, J. and Thomas, C. W. (2011). Quantitative and Qualitative: A Question of Comparability. Extended version of chapter published in International Encyclopedia of Political Science. Eds: Badie, B.; Berg-Schlosser, D.; Morlino, L.; Sage, 2011.

can explain differences in happiness with some explanatory factors, then we may assume that there is causal comparability, and if there is causal comparability, then there must be descriptive comparability. The implication is not that the standards people apply are identical, but that they are similar enough to create comparability.

The fact that happiness is also based on the adoption and adaptation of standards implies that happiness is not a value-free phenomenon.[23] Happiness is not by definition based on virtues or morally acceptable, since people may adopt immoral and egocentric standards in their appreciation of life. Even if happiness is not a value-free phenomenon, however, we can still do happiness research in a value-free fashion. The idea of value-free research was defended by the German sociologist Max Weber.[24] This idea implies, in a nutshell, that the selection of a topic and the formulation of research-questions can never be value-free, because these steps depend on personal or political values. Value-free research is possible, however, in the next stages of any research, and in particular in the collection and analysis of data. If this is done appropriately, then we may expect that different scientists will get the same results.[25] We may assume that this idea is consistent with the vision of David Hume, that we must make a distinction between 'is' and 'ought'.

## Ambition: Less Confusion in Personal and Political Deliberations

Inspired by David Hume and Max Weber, some results of value-free empirical happiness research will be used to reduce the confusion. We may say that happiness is a ***wicked problem***, and we should make it ***less wicked*** by creating more clarity.[26]

[23] In a symposium in Leiden (Netherlands): "*Towards the Wellbeing-Economy*" (December 12, 2019) an economist posed the straight question: "*Who are you to decide what my well-being is?*". He might have asked the same question for happiness. The correct answer would be: "*People are free to decide about their own standards in their evaluation of their own life; and researchers must accept that!*" As a consequence researchers must pay attention to the consistency and stability of the standards and to the diversity of standards of different individuals. If people apply very different standards, their happiness will be dependent on different factors and this creates an interpersonal comparability problem.

[24] Max Weber. Wissenschaft als Beruf (1917–1919) und Politik als Beruf (1919).

[25] This is the generally accepted criterium of the 'repeatability' of research.

[26] Bache, I. and Reardon, L.; (2016) The politics and policy of wellbeing. Edward Elgar Publishing. They define 'wicked problems' as ill-defined problems, without a definitive for-

It is always good to reduce confusion, but there are some specific reasons to reduce the confusion about happiness. The first reason is that happiness is an important type of subjective well-being, and well-being is a central issue in many personal and political deliberations. People, politicians and policy-makers included, spend a lot of time thinking about their own well-being and about well-being in general. It would be beneficial if the reflections and deliberations could be made more effective, by reducing confusion. If we are optimistic, we may even hope that a reduction of confusion can improve the effectiveness of political systems, and may lead to a better management of social conflicts, tensions and problems.

A reduction of confusion will also make it easier to assess the suitability of happiness as a personal or political standard. Happiness is also based on perceived gaps between 'is' and 'ought', and these gaps depend on the adoption and application of standards. We may expect that individuals approve their own standards as a rule. Individual happiness is therefore a natural goal for individuals, but there are complications. The main complication is that individuals adopt many standards unknowingly, and they may adopt inconsistent, overambitious or inconvenient standards, or even immoral standards, for example about racial relations.

It is even less self-evident that we should pursue happiness as a common or collective goal, because individual happiness can, theoretically, be based on very different standards, and might be incomparable as a consequence. It is not helpful to accept happiness as a common goal, if the happiness of every individual is unique.

We have to analyse these problems first before we decide about happiness as a standard, to be used in a descriptive way or to be pursued in our personal life or in politics. The acceptance of happiness as a personal or common standard is ultimately a normative decision. It is appropriate, however, to assess the suitability first, in a value-free fashion, before such decisions are made.

It is important to observe that we can adopt happiness as a standard in different ways. We can accept it in a modest way as a descriptive standard, to describe differences in happiness and to identify and analyse problems. We can also be more ambitious and use happiness as a standard to be actively pursued, and to be used to decide about priorities. If we want to

mulation of the factors involved, without a set of describable solutions, where the explanation determines the nature of the solution. This wicked problem can only be resolved from time to time, but can never be solved for good.

pursue happiness actively, we still have different options. In classical utilitarianism happiness is always pursued in the most effective way: any act or rule contributing the most to average happiness will have the highest priority. In the philosophy of negative utilitarianism, it is the most effective reduction of unhappiness, of the most unhappy people, that will have the highest priority.

Happiness is appreciated as a value in all options, but with different levels of commitment. People who reject happiness as a standard to be actively pursued might still be interested in the application of happiness as a descriptive standard. People can benefit from such exercises by getting a better understanding, even if they are critical about happiness as a dominant goal. It is good to have such options!

## Some Problems of Current Neo-liberalism

It is informative to pay attention to some current social-economic problems that might be identified and analysed more effectively. Neo-liberalism has become a dominant social-economic system in most nations. This neo-liberalism is very successful in many respects, but it goes together with some problems. Happiness as a goal, or just as a standard or point of reference, can make it easier to identify and handle those problems.

Neo-liberalism is based on the pursuit of private interests and directed at maximum utility, as expressed in wealth, individual income and GDP. This is not just selfish or egocentric, but very practical and productive, as explained by Smith. As argued by Sen (1999),[27] there are two basic reasons to respect free markets: first of all as a matter of principle: people should be free to buy and sell, to work and to hire people, to save, and to spend or invest, according to their own priorities. The second reason is that markets are effective in creating employment, a good fit between production and consumption, and a reasonable distribution of labour and other resources. Competition, free trade and mobility of capital, labour and resources are in general beneficial for well-being.[28]

[27] Sen, A. (1999). Development as freedom. Anchor Books, Random House, New York. In particular: Introduction and Chapter 1: The perspective of freedom.

[28] See: Ott, J.C. How much competition do we need in a civilized society? Journal of Happiness Studies, 12(3), 525–529. Review of the book 'Winning; Reflections on an American obsession' (2011) by Francesca Duina. Princeton and Oxford: Princeton University Press.

There is, however, also a broad consensus that free markets can create problems, perhaps as collateral damage, and need effective supervision to manage these problems. Free markets need strong governments to keep them free and effective. Governments must have enough quality, for example sufficient expertise, capability and capacity, to develop policy options, to start a political discussion, and to select options in a democratic way, to provide for adequate interventions. This is particularly important if markets are supposed to deliver crucial commodities and services, like education, energy, water, food, medicine, medical care and financial products. The need for interventions is more complicated if the actual productivity of the economy is high, because then there are more normative choices to be made.

We can make a short tentative list of some current problems of neo-liberalism, which could be identified and analysed more effectively if happiness could be used as a standard.

(a) *In general: frustration of fundamental needs of the poor*

The most general problem with neo-liberalism is that no distinction is made between *fundamental* and *less fundamental* needs. The gratification of needs depends on the availability of money and not on their priority for well-being or happiness. Marginal needs of people with money are gratified quite well, while basic needs of the poor, in particular in poor countries, are not gratified. Rich people can play golf and fly around for their birthday parties, or to lie on beaches for a few days, while poor people do not get adequate medical care and education. This drawback is very clear and visible, but difficult to repair. It might be easier to define and analyse this problem if happiness could be used as an additional standard. The usual economic indicators for progress, like wealth, individual income and GDP, are unfit to deal with such problems. In such indicators expenditures always get the same weight, independent of their impact on well-being or happiness. It is important to notice that the distinction made here, between fundamental and less fundamental needs, deserves critical attention. Rich people may reject the distinction, and may say they really need everything they consume to gratify their needs. They may say they really need nice paintings, for example a Rembrandt, to be happy. Strong arguments are needed to say that such needs are less fundamental than other needs. If we decide to apply happiness as a standard, however, and if the gratification of fundamental needs has more impact on happiness, then we are entitled to put a higher priority on the gratification of fundamental needs.

(b) *Upward pressure on production and consumption*

Neo-liberal capitalism has produced a high level of labour productivity in many nations. This labour productivity is very important for well-being, happiness and individual freedom. This is a great achievement, but some consequences are problematic for happiness and for the sustainability of happiness. Personal income still depends heavily on individual contributions to the production of paid commodities and services. People have to produce to earn money, and their high productivity creates an upward pressure on the production and consumption of paid goods and services. The upward pressure is a problem for ecological sustainability and for the sustainability of happiness. It is also a problem for individual freedom, because it creates a permanent overdose of commercial advertising.

(c) *Security by cost-ineffective positional competition in rich nations*

In neo-liberal societies people always have to put a high priority on their relative financial position in terms of income and wealth, irrespective of the actual quality of their living conditions. High levels of income and wealth always create more security for the gratification of fundamental needs, and in particular against events like illness, disability, unemployment, or being surrounded by bad neighbours. If people can dispose of more money than other people, they can always organize the best medical care and personal support. They can also move to a better neighbourhood if they want to. Some security can be achieved with insurance, but having more money than other people is always the most effective strategy. Efforts to improve relative positions can be beneficial for everybody, if they go together with more productivity, as pointed out by Adam Smith. But this logic becomes disputable if productivity is already at a high level. Improving one's relative financial position, to get more personal security, is very cost-ineffective in high-productivity situations. In such situations improvements in relative positions for some people go together with a deterioration in relative positions for others, without any beneficial side-effects. Collective provisions might be an alternative. We need an additional standard to analyse this problem. Happiness can be such a standard.

(d) *Distribution of work in high-productivity nations*
Particularly in rich nations, with high levels of productivity, neo-liberalism leads to problems in the distribution of work. Levels of income and remuneration are less effective as motivating factors. This is a type of luxury, and we may appreciate this situation, but it creates problems. In rich nations like the Netherlands, it makes it difficult to find people who want to take care of vulnerable young or old people, or people with some disability. A related and symptomatic problem is the tendency of central banks to pump more cheap money into the economy, to keep up economic activity and to minimize unemployment. This random and crude approach is not very effective and leads to low interest rates, with negative consequences for pensions. It also creates more financial inequality, since big banks and rich people benefit disproportionally. In general it leads to less stability and predictability, with detrimental effects for people's ability to make their own plans for the future. They lose control, and losing control is bad for happiness. A better understanding of the pursuit of happiness, as an alternative motivating factor, can make it easier to get the work done, without such kill or cure remedies.

In a nutshell we may conclude that a reduction of confusion about happiness can make it easier to adopt or reject happiness as a personal or collective goal or standard. If we adopt happiness as a personal or collective goal, or just as an additional standard for the evaluation of social-economic situations, it will be easier to identify and analyse current problems. Particularly in rich nations, people are already interested in putting a higher priority on happiness as a standard for social progress, possibly in combination with a lower priority for economic utility-based standards like economic growth and purchasing power. Such a change in priorities in rich nations might create more attention and priority for the low levels of happiness in poor nations. It can also make it easier to diminish questionable consumption and to organize an adequate distribution of labour in rich nations. So far, however, such a change in priorities is not really taking place. Confusion about the meaning, morality and explainability of happiness is an underlying obstacle.

## Approach

The approach in this book is based on the conviction that happiness is an interesting subject, but that we should assess happiness first, as a concept and as an actual phenomenon, before we decide about happiness as a standard to be used in a descriptive way or to be actively pursued. This assessment can be done in a value-free fashion, but the eventual decision is obviously a personal or political choice. Before such a decision is made, we should also try to compare the suitability of happiness as a standard with the suitability of alternative standards, like freedom, justice, solidarity and doing your duty.

The first step in this book is a discussion of the concept of happiness and some characteristics of happiness as a phenomenon (Chap. 2). Chapters 3 and 4 are about affective and cognitive happiness, as the components of overall happiness. In Chap. 5 we get back to overall happiness, as an outcome of the interaction between affective and cognitive happiness. The consistency of overall happiness appears to be sufficient. Chapter 6 is about some results of empirical research. With these results we can assess the comparability of happiness more accurately. Chapter 7 is about the importance of good governance. The relation between governments and citizens is a sensitive issue, but can be managed. Chapter 8 is about arguments to accept or reject happiness as a standard, followed by a careful conclusion. Chapter 9 presents some 'what if' exercises: what might we expect if happiness were accepted as standard in our personal life and in politics? Such exercises are meant to clarify the practical importance of happiness as a standard, and may also stimulate our imagination. Chapter 10 is a summary of the main conclusions.

The first seven chapters are value-free, but the conclusion in Chap. 8 and the 'what if' exercises in Chap. 9 are not value-free. The conclusion of Chap. 8 is that we can use happiness as a standard, and the 'what if' exercises in Chap. 9 are based on the assumption that happiness has at least enough merit to justify such exercises. This conclusion and assumption are obviously not value-free.

My personal/political opinion is that happiness is indeed an acceptable standard. This opinion is based on the inventory of pros and cons, but also on my expectation that a somewhat higher priority for happiness will not have a negative impact on the importance of alternative goals I appreciate, like equality before the law, minimal respect, individual freedom, justice, minimal financial equality and solidarity. It might have a negative effect, however, on the relative importance of economic utility-based goals, like maximal economic growth, personal income, profits and employment just in terms of paid jobs. Such theoretical consequences are acceptable for me. But this is a personal/political conviction about how the world ought to be.

## Title of the Book

There are two reasons for the long title of this book: *Beyond Economics: Happiness as a Standard in our Personal Life and in Politics.* One reason is that the validity of the economic theory of the invisible hand has been eroded by high levels of productivity, and a substantial reduction of scarcity. A second reason is that there are differences between 'utility', as a key concept in economics, and happiness. Happiness is just subjective, utility is somewhat ambiguous because it is subjective, but related to characteristics of goods and services as objective realities, for example the utility of a house is related to the number and the size of the rooms. Utility is about the appreciation of goods and services for sale on the market, as expressed in the prices people are willing to pay, while happiness is about the appreciation of life as a whole. As a consequence happiness has more sources: utility can be derived from the qualities and quantities of goods and services, while happiness can be derived from anything; from goods and services, but also from general conditions, activities, events and social relations. Since happiness depends on more factors, we may conclude that the pursuit of happiness, and the acceptance of happiness as a standard, must go beyond economics.

## Bibliography

Sen, A. (1999). *Development as freedom.* New York: Anchor Books, Random House.

CHAPTER 2

# The Concept and the Nature of Happiness as Subjective Well-Being

## The Current Concept of Happiness and Complications

This chapter presents an explanation of the concept of general or 'overall' happiness with an inventory of some complications. A widely accepted definition of happiness is: *The enduring appreciation of individuals of their own life as a whole.*[1] This appreciation is a mental state, and not by definition based on correct information or high moral standards. Some complications are directly related to the wording in this definition, but there are also some subtle differences between this definition and alternative interpretations in everyday life. The difference between happiness and utility is fundamental and deserves careful consideration. It is also important to pay attention to complications in the nature of happiness as an actual phenomenon; in particular, the subjectivity, the dualism, and the top-down and bottom-up dynamics between happiness and domain satisfactions. First of all we can pose the question of whether we can define happiness, as a specific type of subjective well-being, in a value-free way.

[1] A somewhat more extensive formulation is presented by Veenhoven: *the degree to which an individual judges the overall quality of his/her life-as-a-whole favourably*; or in other words: *how much one likes the life one leads*. Veenhoven, R. In: Introductory text for the World Database of Happiness. Veenhoven, R., *World Database of Happiness*, Erasmus University Rotterdam, The Netherlands. Assessed August 2020 at: http://worlddatabaseofhappiness.eur.nl.


J. Ott, *Beyond Economics*,
https://doi.org/10.1007/978-3-030-56600-5_2

## Happiness, Defined as Subjective Well-Being, Can Be Defined in a Value-Free Way

As very nicely demonstrated by Alexandrova (2017),[2] it is virtually impossible to define well-being in general, without any consideration of the people involved and their social-economic context. If well-being is defined in more specific contexts, then it is, in her view, still impossible to do so in a value-free approach, without the adoption of any value-judgement. These arguments are convincing if well-being, or quality of life for that matter, is defined as an objective reality, with some explicit or implicit selection of standards. Value judgements are indeed inevitable in such definitions.

In a discussion about well-being between economists one economist was therefore fully entitled to pose the straight question: *Who are you to decide what my well-being is?*[3] He might have asked the same question for happiness. People are free, and feel free, to decide about their own individual priorities and standards in their appreciation of their life and living conditions. In this way people are also free to decide how they experience meaning and purpose in life. This is obviously one of the most fundamental capabilities people have.

We do not need such value judgements, however, in the definition of subjective realities. If well-being is defined as a subjective reality, as experienced in people's consciousness, we can just take this experience as a matter of fact. Happiness is a specific type of subjective well-being and can be defined without value-judgements.

## Happiness as a Specific Type of Subjective Well-Being

Ruut Veenhoven (2015)[4] discerns four types of subjective well-being, or well-being as experienced by the people themselves in their consciousness, by making two distinctions, between:

[2] Alexandrova, A. (2017) A philosophy for the science of well-being. Oxford University Press.

[3] In a symposium in Leiden (Netherlands): "*Towards the Wellbeing-Economy*", December 12, 2019.

[4] Veenhoven, R. (2015). Overall satisfaction with life: Subjective approaches. in: Wolfgang Glatzer, Laura Camfield, Valerie Moller & Mariano Rojas (Eds.) 'The Global handbook of Quality of Life: Explorations of well-being in nations and continents', Springer Publishers, Dordrecht, Netherlands, page 207–238.

- Passing short-term subjective well-being and enduring long-term subjective well-being
- Well-being related to specific domains of life or related to life as a whole

The combination of distinctions creates four types of subjective well-being (Table 2.1).

- Passing well-being related to a domain of life: *pleasure*
- Enduring well-being related to a domain of life: *domain satisfaction*
- Passing well-being related to life as a whole: *top experience*
- Enduring well-being related to life as a whole: *happiness*

An interesting issue is the relation between happiness and domain-satisfactions: is happiness an outcome of different domain-satisfactions (bottom-up), or do domain-satisfactions depend on happiness (top-down)? Headey and Wearing (1992, their proposition 3.2)[5] discern seven domains of life, strongly related to happiness or well-being in their terminology: marriage and sex, friendship and leisure, material standard of living, work and health. They find, with Australian panel-data,[6] that happiness has a top-down impact on satisfaction with leisure, material standard of living and work, while there is a mutual influence between happiness and satisfaction with marriage and sex. Health is usually taken for granted and only moderately related to overall happiness. It can become a dissatisfier if there are serious problems; then it has a negative bottom-up impact on overall happiness and on the other domain-satisfactions. Absence of serious health problems is a primary condition for happiness and domain-satisfactions.

**Table 2.1** Four types of subjective well-being; happiness is the enduring appreciation of life as a whole

| | *Passing* | *Enduring* |
|---|---|---|
| Domains of life | *Pleasure* | *Domain satisfaction* |
| Life as a whole | *Top experience* | *Happiness* |

[5] Headey, B. and Wearing, A. (1992). Understanding Happiness: A theory of subjective well-being. Melbourne, Australia. Longman Cheshire Pty Limited.

[6] Source: the Victorian Quality of Life (VQOL) panel study.

## Conceptual Complications Directly Related to the Definition

Happiness is defined as the appreciation of current *life as a whole*. This life has many aspects, like activities, health, events and living conditions. We can also discern domains, like the ones just mentioned. The appreciation is easy if everything is pleasant or unpleasant, but can be complicated if satisfaction is high with some aspects and domains, but low with others.

A second complication is that happiness is about *current life*. People may decide to appreciate their current life with or without any evaluation of their past experiences, and with or without any assessment of their future life. The logical and acceptable assumption is that memories and expectations play a role, if they have some emotional impact on current life.

Another complication is that people may include the well-being of their relatives and friends, or even of the whole world, in their appreciation of their own individual life. How egocentric are people supposed to be in the appreciation of their life? The logical assumption is, here again, that affect can be a referee and that non-egocentric considerations are included if they have some emotional impact. It is wise, however, to pay attention to potential ambiguities, also in the way questions about happiness are formulated.

## Happiness in Colloquial Language in Daily Life

In colloquial language happiness used to be, and sometimes still is, about pleasant events or some perfect state, possibly in the context of some sort of morality.[7] Individuals are supposed to be happy if they experience such pleasant events, or if they have almost or completely reached this perfect state. It is usually not very clear what imagination of a perfect state is used as a frame of reference, either by the observers or by the individuals themselves. The current definition is more specific. Happiness is no longer about some small or substantial difference between a perfect state and reality, but about the *enduring appreciation of individuals of their own life as a whole*. Some imagination of a perfect state can function as a frame of reference, but it is not the appreciation itself.

[7] Philips, J. et al. (2017). True happiness: The role of morality in the folk concept of happiness. Journal of Experimental Psychology. 146(2), 165–181.

Another difference is that in colloquial language people may include specific conditions or reasons for happiness in their definition, for example, happiness is good health, a sense of meaning, purpose and accomplishment, contemplation, a good income or good friends. Some people also find that happiness, as the appreciation of life, must be based on correct information, on virtues and on high moral standards.

In current research such conditions or reasons are usually not included in the definition of happiness. One argument is that such inclusions may prematurely suggest recipes for happiness, by putting too much priority on specific determinants. An additional practical argument is that it would be virtually impossible to assess happiness in empirical research, if such conditions were included in the definition. It is more productive to keep them out, and to define happiness as just the appreciation of life without further constraints. In a further step we can investigate the relations between happiness and such conditions. One trivial consequence of this approach is that the morality of happiness is not self-evident. The standards people apply in the appreciation of their life can be disputable, in view of alternative and perhaps more common standards.

## Happiness and Utility

There are also complications in the interpretation of happiness, because happiness is sometimes mixed up with utility. This is confusing because there are important differences.[8]

'Utility' is a key concept in economics, with an important distinction between expected and experienced utility. People expect a certain utility if they buy commodities or services. This expected utility is expressed in the price they are willing to pay, but their actual experienced utility can be higher or lower.

Happiness and experienced utility are types of subjective well-being, but there are some differences.[9] Happiness is the enduring appreciation of life as a whole as a state of mind. Experienced utility, on the other hand, can also be a short pleasure, related to the fulfilment of specific wants or desires.

[8] Bentham defined utility in terms of happiness.

[9] Ott, J. (2012) Limited experienced happiness or unlimited expected utility, what about the differences? Dissertation 'An Eye on happiness, happiness as an additional goal for citizens and governments', pp. 57–67.

A more fundamental difference is that utility can occasionally refer directly to some objective aspect of goods and services, for example the utility of a car is supposed to depend on the speed and the size of a car, because cars are used for transportation. Experienced utility is therefore subjective, but expected utility, and utility in general, is somewhat ambiguous: subjective but directly related to the characteristics of specific goods and services as objective realities.[10]

There is also a difference in the sources of utility and happiness: utility can be derived from goods and services for sale on the market, but happiness can be derived from anything; not just from goods and services, but also from general living conditions, events, activities and social relations.

Another difference is that utility is unlimited, while happiness is limited, with a minimum and a maximum level. People can always produce and buy more goods and services, and create additional utility. At national level this is reflected in rising national GDP. Utility can therefore be measured with scales without a maximum. Happiness is not unlimited, since it is related to actual experiences and to limited physical and psychological capacities. Happiness is usually measured on scales with a limited number of levels, like 1 to 10.[11]

Happiness is sometimes interpreted as aggregated experienced utility in a certain period (Kahneman 2003),[12] but this is somewhat misleading in view of the differences just mentioned. It is better not to mix up utility and happiness.

Since happiness is limited and related to life as a whole, and since it depends on more factors than goods and services, we may conclude that happiness research must go beyond economics. Happiness is not really an economic issue but is sometimes introduced in economics as an 'external effect'. An external effect is an effect of goods and services, but not reflected in their prices. There are positive and negative external effects; more happiness than reflected in prices is a positive external effect, while less happiness is a negative external effect. This introduction of 'external

[10] It is appropriate here to consider 'The Theory of Moral Sentiments' (Smith, A., first version in 1759; last version in 1790) and in particular Part IV; 'Of the effect of utility upon the sentiment of approbation'. In Smith's vision utility is related to something 'objective', but directly evoking positive (subjective) sentiments.

[11] The measurement of happiness gets more attention in Chap. 6.

[12] Kahneman, D. (2003). Objective Happiness. In D. Kahneman et al. Well-being, the foundation of hedonic psychology. New York: Russell Sage Foundation.

effects' is helpful but insufficient, because it can only be used for goods and services with some price.

We may repeat, finally, that the difference between utility as defined above and happiness was not very substantial in the days of Bentham, because there were scarcities of all kinds of basic products. Utility, as expressed in GDP, income and wealth, therefore contributed to happiness in a very direct and self-evident way. Nowadays we must distinguish these concepts, even if the relation between utility and happiness is still strong in poor nations.[13]

## The Nature of Happiness: A Subjective Reality that Can Be Measured Objectively

In order to understand happiness, we must be familiar with the ontological distinction[14] between 'objective' and 'subjective' realities, and the epistemological distinction[15] between 'objective' and 'subjective' assessments of such realities.

In the previous paragraph happiness is identified as a subjective reality. This is correct, but the distinction between objective and subjective realities is complicated since we also discern the objective and subjective assessment of realities. Perhaps it sounds somewhat academic, but it is worthwhile, for an adequate understanding of happiness, to pay attention to the difference between objective and subjective realities, and to the difference between the objective and subjective assessment of such realities.

[13] The difference between happiness and utility is very visible in the social-economic developments in China. Between 1994 and 2005 real income per capita rose annually on average by 3.7% in rural China and by 5.4% in urban China; but happiness as measured by Gallup, the Asia barometer and the World Values Survey decreased. See Knight, K. and Gunatilaka, Subjective Well-being and Social Evaluation in a Poor Country. CSAE Working Paper WPS/2014-09. See also: Graham, C., Happiness around the World: The Paradox of Happy Peasants and Miserable Millionaires. Oxford: Oxford University Press, 2010.

[14] 'Ontological' is about realities or facts as they are; and we can discern objective realities, independent of the individual consciousness, and subjective realities as experienced in the individual consciousness.

[15] 'Epistemological' is about the way we describe realities; we can do it on the basis of our own personal standards, or we can do it in a way that makes the description independent of our own personal standards.

## The Ontological Distinction Between Objective and Subjective Realities

In an ontological way objective realities exist outside and independent of the human consciousness, while subjective realities exist within, and depend on, the human consciousness. Houses and railroads do exist independent of our consciousness and are objective realities, just like blood pressure, body-temperature, life-expectancy, weight and height. Personality characteristics, like extraversion and neuroticism, are also objective realities. Happiness, pain and pleasure, gratitude, hope, optimism and trust are subjective realities, because they are experienced in our consciousness and cannot exist outside of it.

A dilemma to deal with is whether we want to define 'the human consciousness' as 'an individual consciousness' or as 'human consciousness in general'. In my view we should focus on the individual consciousness, since this is the actual place where subjective realities like happiness can be found.[16] This choice may create some odd and confusing terminology occasionally: collective subjective realities, like common cultural values and expectations, are objective realities because they exist independent of anyone's individual consciousness. For the people who share them, such realities are both objective and subjective, but for people who do not share them, they are objective only. They can only become subjective realities if people adopt or 'internalize' them, knowingly or unknowingly.

Objective realities can become subjective realities if they are important and get enough attention. Safety and health are objective realities independent of our consciousness. But our own safety and health, or the safety and health of people we care about, can also become subjective realities, if they play a prominent role in our individual consciousness. People obviously think and communicate about such important objective realities, and develop opinions, ideas and feelings as subjective realities. The mass media play an important role in this process. The relation between objective and subjective realities is not self-evident: people can be safe objectively, but feel unsafe subjectively, and it can be the other way around as well.

[16] Tim Taylor in his book "Knowing What is Good For You" (2012, Palgrave Macmillan, pp. 19–20) distinguishes broad and narrow senses of 'subjective'. Such things as common cultural values might be seen as subjective in a broad sense, being dependent upon the human mind at *some* level. But in discussing individual happiness and well-being, it is appropriate to use a narrower sense, in which what is subjective is dependent upon the mental states *of the individual concerned*.

A related complication in research is that researchers sometimes try to measure objective realities by asking people about their perception of such realities. This approach is problematic if people are not really familiar with the objective realities; then their perceptions can be based on hearsay or wishful thinking. Then the researchers might end up measuring subjective instead of objective realities, Measuring crime, for example corruption, is a well-known example: if researchers measure corruption by asking people about their perception of corruption in their country, they might just be measuring perceptions instead of actual corruption. But asking for perceptions can be an adequate approach if the perceptions are related to regular events or behaviour people know about; for example, how many times on a day do you leave your home usually? Here again: the relation between objective and subjective is not self-evident.

The distinction between subjective and objective realities is important because subjective realities are elements in psychological dynamics, with an important role for genetic factors, emotional development and personality. Objective realities are not dependent on such dynamics. It is not by definition easier or more complicated to change subjective instead of objective realities, but it may take different interventions to do so.

## The Epistemological Distinction Between Objective and Subjective Assessments of Realities

Epistemology is not about reality itself but about the way people observe, describe and assess reality. Assessments are subjective in an epistemological way if they depend on the personal characteristics or the taste of the observers. Tall and heavy people may find that other people are rather short and slim. Optimistic people may find that other people are somewhat pessimistic. Such assessments are subjective, because they depend on the tastes and characteristics of the observers. Objective assessments can be organized by making the assessments independent of such individual tastes and characteristics, for example by using a weighing scale for weight and a tape-measure for height. This objectivity can also be achieved by the application of standard procedures. Asking standardized survey questions in a standardized manner is a well-known option. The test for objectivity is that the results are the same if the assessment procedures are applied by different people.

## Objective and Subjective Well-Being as Realities

Objective well-being is well-being outside our consciousness, in terms of objective realities like income, life-expectancy, wealth, social contacts, and objective safety and health. The possibilities to define objective well-being are unlimited. Subjective well-being, on the other hand, is well-being as experienced by the people themselves in their consciousness. The possibilities to define subjective well-being are not unlimited, because it all depends on actual subjective experiences.

## Objective and Subjective Well-Being; Objectively or Subjectively Measured

We can discern four situations in the assessment of well-being if we apply the distinction 'objective-subjective' simultaneously in an ontological and epistemological way.

(a) Somebody can assess someone else's objective well-being in a subjective way in terms of personal impressions, like 'I think he is rich' or 'I think she is healthy'.
(b) Somebody can assess someone's objective well-being in an objective way, for example, by applying indicators like income, wealth, blood pressure, body-mass-index.
(c) Somebody can assess someone's subjective well-being in a subjective way in terms of personal impressions, like 'I think she is happy', or 'I think he is optimistic and hopeful'.
(d) Somebody can assess someone's subjective well-being in an objective way, for example, by asking standardized questions in a survey, about contentment or happiness. There are options for doing this without asking questions, like assessing facial expressions (do people smile?) or MRI-research (use of oxygen in parts of the brains), but such methods are not very precise. Standard survey questions, asked in identical ways and conditions, are usually used to assess subjective well-being in an objective way.

The difference between objective and subjective well-being is important, because objective well-being is directly related to actual and visible living conditions, while subjective well-being is related to what people experience in their consciousness. Subjective realities in our consciousness are interdependent because they are elements in fundamental psychological dynamics, with some common causes like genes and personality. An important question in happiness research is whether happiness depends primarily on subjective realities, like optimism and trust, or on objective realities, like income and objective safety and health. The answer is obviously important if we want to promote happiness in our personal life or in politics.

## Subjective and Objective Indicators of Well-Being

Since we may assume that assessments in scientific research are always objective in an epistemological way (b or d above), we may also assume that in scientific publications the qualifications 'subjective' and 'objective' usually refer to the ontological distinction between objective and subjective realities. This is certainly true for the distinctions between subjective and objective well-being and between subjective and objective indicators. Subjective indicators are used to assess subjective well-being (as experienced in the consciousness) and objective indicators are used to assess objective well-being (independent of the individual consciousness).

Happiness is a special type of subjective well-being. Standardized survey questions to measure happiness in an objective way are therefore subjective indicators! Self-reported happiness, in response to such standardized survey questions, is subjective in an ontological way but objectively measured in an epistemological way.

## The Nature of Happiness: Dualism of Affect and Cognition

Another basic characteristic of happiness, with conceptual confusion, is that overall happiness has two components: the affective component with emotions and moods as elements, and the cognitive component, with thoughts and judgements as elements.

It is important to distinguish between short- and long-term affective happiness. Short-term affective happiness, sometimes denoted as hedonic level of affect, consists of emotions and moods. The difference between emotions and moods is that emotions get more attention in our consciousness, because they are more specific and more straightforwardly positive or negative. Emotions are therefore better memorized than moods, but are not by definition more important. Usually we just refer to emotions for shortness. Long-term affective happiness consists of more enduring emotional dispositions like cheerfulness and pessimism. Such dispositions are related to emotional experiences in the past, but also to personality and genetic characteristics.

Frustration or gratification of needs will always yield negative or positive emotions respectively, but the more chronic and prominent negative emotions are usually related to the previous or current frustration of fundamental needs, like the need for recognition and physical and social safety. Positive and negative emotions are also related to perceived gaps between how things actually are and how they 'should be' and to fundamental individual characteristics, like personality, genes and objective health, for example levels of neurotransmitters.

Cognitive happiness, sometimes denoted as contentment, is an evaluation of one's life as a whole, after some 'thinking' or 'reflection', and is based on the application of standards, or sets of standards in frames of reference. Instead of the phrase *standards* we may also use alternative expressions with some normative connotation as equivalents like *indicator*, *criterion*, *measure*, *norm*, *demand*, *expectation*, *goal* and *value*. There is always some normative connotation or loading, but in slightly different degrees; going up from *indicator* to *value*. *Standard* and *norm* are somewhere in the middle. It is important to notice that people may adopt and apply *standards* unknowingly, and may have them without being aware of it.

Cognitive happiness depends on people's perception of their own achievements and their own social position. It may also depend on perceived gaps between how the world really is and how it should be according to their standards and expectations. People may have strong emotions about such gaps, so at this point there is a clear connection between affective and cognitive happiness. Affective as well as cognitive happiness can be problematic if the standards people apply are very ambitious or inconsistent.

Affective and cognitive happiness have their own dynamics and are occasionally denoted as specific types of happiness in their own kind. This creates the tripartite terminology of *overall, cognitive and affective happiness.* This typology, based on differences in underlying dynamics, is very common and will be followed in the next chapters, but in view of some research findings, we may also consider a somewhat different typology in Chap. 6.

## Why Do People Have an Enduring Appreciation of Their Own Life as a Whole?

It is perhaps the most spectacular finding of happiness research, also in view of all these conceptual complications, that most people are able to answer simple survey questions about their overall happiness. The percentage 'Don't know' or 'No Answer' is in general very low. This is remarkable, because people have to make several awkward decisions if they want to answer such survey questions. They must decide whether they want to take into account their social and physical environment, the well-being of friends and relatives, their past experiences and their expectations for the future. They also have to decide about the importance of their living conditions and their priorities for affect and cognitive evaluation.

Children will automatically put a high priority on affect, because their cognitive evaluation is still 'under construction'. If children or adults assess their affective happiness, then they have to memorize what emotions and moods have been dominant recently. Adults may decide whether they want to put priority on their affective or cognitive happiness. If they put priority on cognitive evaluation, they have to decide about standards. They may even apply moral, political, religious or ethical standards in the appreciation of their life as a whole, if they feel inclined to do so.

If everything is clearly positive or negative it is obviously easy to answer happiness questions, but in many situations it will be complicated. It is therefore amazing that people usually answer survey questions in a reliable and rational way.[17] One explanation is that people value happiness[18] and think a lot about their *life as a whole* for good reasons.[19] One good reason is that it is practical and convenient to have some provisional answer available about overall happiness. A provisional answer can make it easier to decide swiftly and adequately about new opportunities and dilemmas. And a provisional answer can be a convenient starting point for more specific considerations and discussions.

[17] Diener, E. (1994) Assessing Subjective Well-Being: Progress and Opportunities. Social Indicators Research, 31, 103–157.

[18] People value happiness: Abrams, M., Gerard, T. Timms, N. (1985). Values and social change in Britain. Macmillan, London.

[19] People think about how satisfied or happy they are with their lives at least every week if not every day: Dalkey, N. C. (1973). Studies in the quality of life. Lexington Books, Lexington.

Overall happiness, as the appreciation of life as a whole, is therefore more than just a passive ex post appreciation of life; it can also function as a compass or radar, and as input for new social-psychological developments. People may even try to be positive about their life as a strategy, because this may work as a self-fulfilling prophecy.[20] This tendency to develop an overall appreciation of life as a whole can facilitate a top-down effect: if people have an overall appreciation of their life as a whole, they can use this appreciation as a starting point in their appreciation of different domains.

## Happiness Is Dynamic Between a Maximum and Minimal Level

In research happiness is supposed to have a minimum and a maximum level, at specific moments or as an average over longer periods. This is a justification for using scales, for example a 1–10 scale. This assumption is consistent with the basic idea that there is a natural range for negative and positive emotions in affective happiness. For thoughts and judgements in cognitive evaluations, this is perhaps less self-evident. It is acceptable, however, in view of the fact that many people apply frames of reference, defining some specific best possible, and some specific worst possible life. A related argument is that happiness may have an informative and even strategic function, and for such functions it is sufficient to have some minimum and maximum level, with an informative range of levels in between. We do not need unlimited happiness, or unlimited unhappiness, to take better decisions.

The assumption that happiness has a maximum level is obviously important if we want to understand the relations between happiness and actual conditions. If individuals reach their maximum level of happiness, or if average happiness in nations is close to some natural maximum, then we cannot expect that any new improvements in living conditions will be

[20] Voltaire once said: "I decided to be happy, because it is better for my health." An interesting outcome of research in this context is that florists are happier than bankers. (Found in Dolan, P. Happiness by Design, p. 77 (2014). Penguin Books; source: Career Happiness Index 2012.) Perhaps it is more important for florists than for bankers to be happy in their contacts with clients. This might be just a matter of keeping up appearances, but might have a real impact on actual happiness eventually.

reflected in more happiness.[21] The implication is not, however, that such improvements are irrelevant for happiness. Improvements in actual conditions can still make happiness more robust, and less vulnerable for adversity. The Corona-pandemic in 2020 made it very clear again, that well-organized societies do a better job in the protection of well-being and happiness. It is easier to maintain high levels of well-being and happiness, if the conditions are good enough to react adequately.

Happiness has a maximum level, and it is a dynamic phenomenon because it depends on perceived gaps between the world as it is and how it should be, in view of expectations. Happiness can go down if expectations go up. If progress is interpreted as a linear development, going up all the time and without a maximum, then happiness is perhaps less suitable as a standard. We will have to pay attention to these characteristics of happiness, if we want to use it as a goal or standard to be pursued.

## Ordinal Level Perhaps More Realistic, But Interval Level Is Acceptable

If we use numbers to describe some reality, we must adopt certain assumptions. If we measure weight or height, the difference between 80 and 83 kilo is assumed to be the same as between 50 and 53 kilo, and the difference between 20 and 23 inch is assumed to be the same as between 40 and 43 inch. This assumption of 'equidistance' is necessary if we want to work in a meaningful way with an average. In happiness this assumption is debatable; the difference between 2 and 3 on a scale for self-reported happiness probably represents something different as the difference between 7 and 8. Van Praag and Ferrer-i-Carbonell (2004)[22] found, however, that we can nevertheless work with this assumption in happiness research, without making serious mistakes.

The fact that happiness may have an informative/cybernetic, and occasionally even a strategic function, is an additional argument to accept

[21] Easterlin found that economic growth has no substantial impact anymore on happiness in rich nations. If such nations have (almost) reached their 'natural' maximum, then this can be one of the explanations. In: Easterlin, R. (1974). Does economic growth improve the human lot? Some empirical evidence. In David, P.A. & Reder, W. (Eds.) Nations and households in economic growth: Essays in honour of Moses Abramowitz. New York, NY, Academic Press.

[22] Van Praag, B., Ferrer-i-Carbonell, A. (2004). Happiness quantified. A satisfaction calculus approach, Oxford University Press.

interval measurement. It is convenient for people, in view of these functions, to rate their happiness on a scale with an informative range of levels with a certain continuity. Going up or down the range, on a scale with a minimum and maximum, should reflect a gradual development without any drastic or critical dividing lines. It is therefore acceptable that happiness is usually measured at interval level.

## Internal Consistency and Comparability of Overall Happiness

Overall happiness is consistent if there are no serious inconsistencies, for example, between affective and cognitive happiness, or between the standards people apply in their appreciation of life. There is a strong interaction between affect and cognition, with strong tendencies towards consistency. There can be inconsistencies nevertheless, because there are regular and substantial fluctuations in short-term affective happiness, while cognitive happiness is rather stable. If the inconsistencies are serious, people will have to think carefully about their overall appreciation of their life as a whole. If they cannot decide about their overall appreciation, the simple conclusion is that for them there is no such thing as 'overall happiness'. Usually people are able to decide. We have to keep in mind, however, that they may decide, even if there are serious inconsistencies, because it is convenient to have some encompassing appreciation of life as a whole.

If people have this appreciation, there is still the further issue of the comparability of individual overall happiness. The first question is: can we compare the self-reported happiness of different people in the same periods of time? This question is about the 'interpersonal comparability' of happiness. The second question is: can we compare the self-reported happiness of the same people in different periods of time? This question is about the stability and 'longitudinal comparability' of happiness.

Interpersonal comparability depends primarily on the diversity of the standards people apply in their appreciation of life as a whole. If they apply the same or similar standards, we may expect interpersonal comparability. The longitudinal comparability depends on the stability of such standards. We may expect longitudinal comparability if people maintain the same or similar standards over longer periods of time. The interpersonal or longitudinal comparability can be very poor, at least theoretically, if there is substantial diversity and instability in the standards. It is wise to have a look at the specific dynamics of affective and cognitive happiness first, before we try to assess the consistency and comparability of overall happiness.

## Bibliography

Alexandrova, A. (2017). *A philosophy for the science of well-being*. Oxford: Oxford University Press.

Headey, B., & Wearing, A. (1992). *Understanding happiness: A theory of subjective well-being*. Melbourne: Longman Cheshire Pty Limited.

Van Praag, B., & Ferrer-i-Carbonell, A. (2004). *Happiness quantified. A satisfaction calculus approach*. Oxford: Oxford University Press.

CHAPTER 3

# Affective Happiness, or the Affective Component of Happiness

## Emotions and Moods: General Function and Comparability

Emotions and moods are the elements of short-term affective or experiential happiness; emotional dispositions like cheerfulness or pessimism are elements in long-term affective happiness. Emotions are more straightforwardly positive or negative than moods and get more attention in our consciousness. For brevity we usually just mention emotions as the elements of affective happiness. Ad Bergsma (1995,[1] inspired by Frijda 1988)[2] discerns some characteristics of emotions.

1. Emotions are important in the relations between individuals and their physical or social environment. Positive emotions indicate that things are going in the right direction, while negative emotions indicate that things are going in the wrong direction. Emotions are therefore important elements in the appreciation of life as a whole, even if they can be illogical and irrational. The qualifications *positive*, *negative*, *good* and *bad* are no judgements of value in this context,

[1] Bergsma, A. (1995). Emoties en kwaliteit van bestaan, (Emotions and quality of life) Het Spectrum, Utrecht.

[2] Frijda, N. (1988). De emoties; een overzicht van onderzoek en theorie. (The emotions; a review of research and theory) Amsterdam, Bert Bakker.


J. Ott, *Beyond Economics*,
https://doi.org/10.1007/978-3-030-56600-5_3

but reflect the way emotions are experienced by the people themselves.

2. Emotions are primarily related to changes in situations, and less to the quality of situations as such. People get used to situations and then the emotional impact of the situation will be low. Bergsma observes that this is a basic characteristic of the nervous system. If a sensorial cell gets a permanent stimulation, then the sensitivity of the cell will diminish, while this sensitivity will remain high at lower levels of stimulation. In this respect people get used to situations, but it takes more time to get used to negative emotions than to positive emotions.
3. Strong emotions never vanish completely; they stay around somewhere in the human mind, and can return to the foreground if people are somehow reminded of the conditions or events that originally produced them. This is, unfortunately, also the case for strong negative emotions, as in post-traumatic stress disorder. It is also interesting that specific events or conditions can provoke emotions because they have some symbolic meaning or importance. This is perhaps even more so for social events and conditions, like parties and festivities.
4. Emotions are important motivational forces for individuals. Pain and pleasure motivate people to deal with problems and to look for benefits and opportunities. Emotions provoke action.
5. Emotions have a strong interaction with cognition. Cognition creates a context for the interpretation of situations and events. Without any interaction, it would even be debatable whether affective happiness has anything to do with the appreciation of life. Without interpretation, emotions would just be products of the gratification or frustration of needs, without any meaning. Positive emotions are not by definition appreciated and negative emotions are not by definition deplorable. Such interpretations have an impact on the intensity of emotions. People are aware of their emotions and can reflect on them. Emotions are important starting points for thoughts and judgements.
6. Most emotions are not illogical or irrational but related to the frustration or gratification of general needs. Specific emotions are even automatic and predictable. People get angry at an offence, sad when losing something valuable and anxious in dangerous or threatening situations.

There are convincing arguments that human emotions are universal. Emotions are not learned but innate, and essentially independent of culture and nurture. Even children who grow up just by themselves, without any contact with any other people, have the usual basic emotions like joy, sorrow and anger. Facial expressions of basic emotions are universal and generally recognized, even if the public expression of emotions can be different in different cultures. One underlying reason for the universality of emotions is that the gratification or frustration of universal human needs is an important source.

## Mild Positive Emotions Can Go Together with Mild Negative Emotions

One of the interesting results of happiness research, mentioned in the previous chapter, is that up to a point positive emotions can go together with relatively mild negative emotions. As found by Headey and Wearing (1992, their proposition 6.1), people can combine feelings of happiness and satisfaction with mild negative feelings of anxiety.[3] The combination of happiness with more serious negative feelings, like feelings of depression, is more problematic. Following Diener (1985),[4] they discern the frequency and the intensity of emotions. The frequencies of mild positive and negative feelings can be high in a specific period, because mild positive and mild negative emotions can go together. This is different for emotions with a high intensity: then the negative emotions will overrule the positive emotions or vice versa.

Headey and Wearing found (their proposition 6.3) that some domains of life, like friendships and leisure, are more related to positive feelings than to negative feelings. Good health is usually taken for granted, but serious health problems produce strong negative feelings. Other domains, like marriage, work and the material standard of living, are equally strongly related to positive and negative feelings.

[3] Headey, B. and Wearing, A. (1992). Understanding Happiness: A theory of subjective well-being. Melbourne, Australia. Longman Cheshire Pty Limited.

[4] Diener, E., Larsen, L.J., Levine, S. and Emmons, R. A. (1985) Intensity and Frequency: Dimensions underlying positive and negative affect. Journal of Personality and Social Psychology, vol. 48, pp. 1253–65.

## General Human Needs

Veenhoven (2009)[5] discerns general *innate needs* from learned *wants.* This is an important distinction. People have the same needs but their needs are gratified in different ways. People have to eat, but what and how they eat depends on their cultural and individual wants. Wants are more specific and related to the actual availability of options. In this respect wants are comparable with preferences, even though they can be more general and less related to specific commodities or services. Wants and preferences are obviously related to needs, but can be manipulated while innate needs are unchangeable. Manipulated wants and preferences may even be inconsistent with innate needs.[6]

According to Veenhoven, happiness depends first of all on the gratification or frustration of needs. Gratification or frustration of needs leads to positive and negative emotions. Such emotions are elements in affective happiness, or in the affective component of overall happiness, occasionally also denoted as 'the hedonic level of affect'. Moods are also elements in this affective happiness, but are less straightforwardly positive or negative, and the awareness of moods is usually somewhat lower.

Maslow (1943)[7] discerns seven needs:

1. Physiological needs
2. Need for safety and security for the future, includes job and financial security and absence of discrimination
3. Need for love and belonging
4. Need for esteem (recognition, minimal respect, no discrimination)
5. Cognitive needs, curiosity, need for new stimuli
6. Aesthetic needs for beauty, structure and art
7. Need for self-actualization

[5] Veenhoven, R. (2009) How do we assess how happy we are? Tenets, implications and tenability of three theories'. Ii: Dutt, A. K. & Radcliff, B. (eds.) 'Happiness, Economics and Politics: Towards a multi-disciplinary approach', Edward Elger Publishers, Cheltenham UK, Chapter 3, page 45–69.

[6] See Ott, J.C. (2006). Do not trust your own wants if you want to be happy! Journal of Happiness Studies, 7 (4), 517–522; Review of the book Happiness; the science behind your smile (2005) by Daniel Nettle, UK; Oxford University Press.

[7] Maslow, A.H. (1943). A Theory of Human Motivation. Psychological Review 50(4): 370–396.

The Dutch social psychologist Wentholt (1980) developed a typology of motivations, related to a comparable typology of general needs.[8]

1. Motivations based on homeostatic regulation:

(a) Internal physiological regulation (the need to maintain body temperature)
(b) Hunger, thirst (need for food)
(c) Sexuality (need for a partner)
(d) The emergency motivations: aggression and fear (need for safety, minimal respect included, since this is a condition for safety)

2. Motivations based on stimulus-seeking:

(a) Affection (need for intimacy and social/psychological support)
(b) Intrinsic motivation, directed at the development of capabilities (need for appropriate challenges)

This last motivation in Wentholt's typology, the intrinsic motivation related to the need for appropriate challenges, is important for the gratification of cognitive needs and the need for self-actualization in Maslow's typology. This intrinsic motivation is very visible if we look at playing children or dogs. This intrinsic motivation is important for the development of capabilities.

## Hierarchy of Needs?

Maslow once proclaimed that there is a general hierarchy in his typology of needs, meaning that, going up from one to seven, 'lower' needs have to be gratified first, before 'higher' needs can be gratified. There is, as Maslow admitted later, no empirical support for such a general hierarchy. People are willing and able to neglect the gratification of lower needs and to put a higher priority on the gratification of higher needs. Some people who believe in some idealistic purpose can accept a lot of suffering, and can sacrifice almost everything they have, to pursue this purpose. The gratification of some need is certainly not fully dependent on the gratification of lower needs.

[8]Wentholt, R. (1980). Motivation Theory. Unpublished Reader. Erasmus University Rotterdam, Netherlands.

There are, however, strong arguments to assume that there is a more specific hierarchy, in the sense that the needs related to safety and security are more important for happiness than the other needs. The second need identified by Maslow is explicitly about safety and security, but his first need, the need of gratification of physiological needs, is also crucial in this respect. Even his third and fourth needs, those for belonging and esteem, with elements like recognition, minimal respect and absence of discrimination, are crucial. People are social animals and cannot live an acceptable life without reasonable social relations.

A distinction between the first four fundamental needs, and the less fundamental cognitive and aesthetic needs and the need for self-actualization, is therefore justifiable. The qualification *fundamental* is not a judgement of value in this context, but reflects the fact that the gratification of some needs has more impact on emotional development and happiness over the life course.

One argument is that these first four needs are always important, starting from birth and independent of age, while the last three needs can only develop at later age, and only if the previous emotional development has been good enough. This is consistent with the observation of Barbara Fredrickson, that positive emotions facilitate personal development,[9] while intense negative emotions are an obstacle. This observation supports the need to distinguish between emotions and moods at specific moments and over longer periods. Safety and security are obviously crucial conditions in this respect.

A second argument is that the first four needs are more coercive in difficult situations, as in war or in case of natural disasters. The needs for safety and security, for example for shelter, food and minimal respect, will get a higher priority in such situations. The difference is less obvious if such fundamental needs are gratified in 'normal' situations, but this is no excuse to ignore the difference. If there is an emergency situation, or if people believe they are in such a situation, fundamental needs related to safety will get higher priorities.

This conclusion would be rather theoretical if objective emergency situations were virtually non-existent, and if people never subjectively felt themselves to be in such situations. But emergency situations do occur, and even if they do not occur in some objective way, people may feel

[9] Frederickson, B.L. (2001). The role of positive emotions in positive psychology: The broaden-and-build theory of positive emotions. American Psychologist, 56 (3), 218–226.

threatened by perceived threats. Unreasonable inequality and discrimination can create real threats for physical and social safety, and can also create such perceptions.

If the fundamental or basic needs are more important for happiness over the life course, and if we accept happiness as a goal or standard, then the gratification of these needs deserves a higher priority than the gratification of other needs. This is an important conclusion.

## Special Importance of the Need for Safety

The frustration of fundamental needs related to safety and security has very negative effects, not just for the people whose needs are frustrated, but also for the people in their environment and society as a whole. If people feel unsafe, they can become aggressive and anxious. If they feel unsafe for longer periods, for example if they are raised or live in unsafe or unfair conditions, then their aggressiveness and anxiety can become permanent attitudes. People can become aggressive or anxious independently of any actual threats, and without any objective justification.

Feeling safe depends also on minimal respect. Minimal respect is important, because people need some security that they will be treated carefully, respectfully and without discrimination. High levels of unreasonable and conspicuous inequality, corruption and discrimination can provoke negative developments, with a negative impact on subjective safety and happiness (Wilkinson 2005[10]; Stiglitz 2012,[11] Graham 2017[12]). Showing respect for fundamental needs of other people, on the other hand, is always appreciated and is always an effective way to develop constructive and rewarding social relations.

## Special Importance of the Need for Appropriate Challenges

The need for appropriate challenges, to use and develop capabilities, also deserves some additional attention. If there are serious problems with the gratification of fundamental needs, then there is obviously no need for any

[10] Wilkinson, R.. (2005). The impact of inequality: how to make sick societies healthier. Routledge; London.

[11] Stiglitz, J. (2012). The price of inequality. W.W. Norton & Company. New York.

[12] Graham, C. (2017). Happiness for all? Princeton University Press. New Jersey.

additional challenges. If the fundamental problems are solved, and people no longer have to worry about their physical and social safety, then there is room for additional challenges. Challenges are more important for children, because they need nice and appropriate challenges to develop their capabilities. We have to acknowledge, however, that even for children, safety and security deserve a higher priority than the need for challenges. Children and adults are not interested in additional challenges if they have to deal with danger and insecurity.

The implication is that inactivity is, in general, bad for happiness; people usually want to be active, unless they are exhausted or troubled with serious physical or mental problems. If fundamental needs, like the need for safety and security, are gratified, people will try to find new challenges that fit their personal capabilities and convictions. If they are safe and relatively rich, they will have some freedom in the selection of such challenges.

## Stepping Stones to Cognition: Awareness of Emotions, Identity, Living Conditions and Inconsistencies

The motivations in Wentholt's typology are organic and similar for people and animals. The highly developed human consciousness, however, based on the availability of language, has a tremendous impact on the way motivations and underlying needs are assessed and gratified. Wentholt (1980)[13] discerns the following typical content of the human consciousness:

(a) Awareness of emotions
(b) Awareness of one's own identity
(c) Awareness of existential (living) conditions
(d) Awareness of cognitive inconsistencies

This basic content of the human consciousness, developed in childhood, is important for affective and cognitive happiness. The awareness of emotions obviously facilitates the interaction between affect and cognition, but is also important because emotions are informative. Emotions can be consequences of pleasant or unpleasant events, or of objective physiological conditions of the body, for example some disease like flu,

[13] Wentholt, R. (1980). Motivation Theory. Unpublished Reader. Erasmus University Rotterdam, Netherlands.

hormonal unrest, problems with neurotransmitters and adrenalin. But emotions can also be consequences of perceived gaps between reality and normative convictions about how things should be.

It can be difficult to identify the real reasons for negative or positive emotions, but if people develop some understanding, it will be easier for them to set priorities and to take decisions. In this respect we may say that both affective and cognitive happiness have a useful 'cybernetic'[14] function; they represent information about harmony or disharmony between needs and actual living conditions, to be used as input for decisions.

The awareness of emotions, of one's own identity and personal living conditions, stimulates people to think about their achievements and their individual position. As a consequence they will try to develop theories about their individual position and their life as a whole. The so-called awareness of cognitive inconsistencies may stimulate them to avoid such inconsistencies, if it is possible to do so. In this way they can develop consistent theories about the world around them, their personal position and their achievements.

It is very functional to have such theories, because they facilitate swift and adequate decisions, for example about buying a house, finding a partner or a job, having children and getting involved in politics. The 'cybernetic' functions of affective and cognitive happiness explain why people think a lot about their happiness, as the appreciation of their lives as a whole, and why people are in general quite able to answer survey questions about happiness. Thinking about happiness is useful because it will make it easier to take decisions and to deal with problems and opportunities.

The cybernetic function may also imply that happiness is more than just a passive appreciation of life; it may imply that happiness has some strategic aspect. In a nutshell: thinking about happiness will make it easier to pursue happiness effectively.

## Comparability of Affective Happiness?

We will consider the comparability of overall happiness later, but it is helpful to look briefly at the comparability of affective happiness. Affective happiness of different individuals, or of the same individuals at different moments, is probably comparable, at least in as far as it depends on the

[14] Cybernetics: the science of communication and control.

gratification of the same general human needs. We have to keep in mind, however, that affective happiness, and long-term affective happiness in particular, also depends on individual characteristics related to personality and genetics. Individual differences in such characteristics may have an adverse effect on the comparability. We also have to keep in mind that affective happiness depends on perceived gaps between 'is' and 'ought', and people perceive different gaps. These gaps are elements in cognitive happiness but with emotional consequences. It is wise, therefore, to have a closer look at the specific dynamics of cognitive happiness.

## Bibliography


Bergsma, A. (1995). *Emoties en kwaliteit van bestaan [Emotions and quality of life]*. Utrecht: Het Spectrum.

Diener, E., Larsen, L. J., Levine, S., & Emmons, R. A. (1985). Intensity and frequency: Dimensions underlying positive and negative affect. *Journal of Personality and Social Psychology, 48*, 1253–1265.

Frijda, N. (1988). *De emoties; een overzicht van onderzoek en theorie [The emotions; a review of research and theory]*. Amsterdam: Bert Bakker.

Graham, C. (2017). *Happiness for all?* Princeton, NJ: Princeton University Press.

Maslow, A. H. (1943). A theory of human motivation. *Psychological Review, 50*(4), 370–396.

Stiglitz, J. (2012). *The price of inequality*. New York: W.W. Norton & Company.

Veenhoven, R. (2009). *How do we assess how happy we are?* Tenets, implications and tenability of three theories'. In A. K. Dutt & B. Radcliff (Eds.), *Happiness, economics and politics: Towards a multi-disciplinary approach*. Cheltenham: Edward Elgar Publishers, Chapter 3, pp. 45–69.

Wentholt, R. (1980). *Motivation theory*. Unpublished reader. Erasmus University Rotterdam, Rotterdam.

Wilkinson, R. (2005). *The impact of inequality: How to make sick societies healthier*. London: Routledge.

CHAPTER 4

# Cognitive Happiness, or the Cognitive Component of Happiness

## Introduction: The Nature of Cognitive Happiness

Thoughts, judgements and standards are important elements in cognitive happiness, sometimes denoted as evaluative happiness, contentment, or life-satisfaction. Cognitive happiness is an evaluation of one's life as a whole, after some thinking or reflection, and is based on the application of standards, or combinations of standards, in frames of reference. Instead of the phrase *standards*, we may also use alternative expressions with some normative connotation as equivalents, like *indicator*, *criterion*, *measure*, *norm*, *demand*, *expectation*, *goal* and *value*. There is, as mentioned before, always some normative connotation or loading, but in slightly different degrees; going up from *indicator* to *value*.

It is unusual to assume that human life as a whole is subordinated to some higher purpose, even if there is a tendency to do so in some religions. The appreciation of our life as a whole is therefore unrelated to some functionality or instrumentality and requires the adoption and application of autonomous normative standards.

The situation is somewhat different for *preferences*, an important concept in economics. Preferences are related to the practical options people have, like buying available commodities and services. Such commodities and services have some well-known functionality or instrumentality and can be appreciated in a practical or technical way, without too much normative consideration. Normative standards and preferences are sometimes


J. Ott, *Beyond Economics*,
https://doi.org/10.1007/978-3-030-56600-5_4

used as equivalents, but this is only correct if preferences have a normative meaning, independent of any functionality or instrumentality. Preferences are comparable with wants. Preferences and wants are usually related to the innate general needs, but are not by definition consistent with these needs.

## Fundamental and Less Fundamental Standards

There are all kinds of standards, for example practical standards about food, sports, physical appearance, hygiene, art, music, how to behave in public and many other aspects of daily life. But there are also more fundamental standards about how to interact with other people, in terms of morality, sympathy, trust, justice, duty, solidarity and individual freedom. Compliance with such fundamental standards is important for the experience of meaning and purpose. Many philosophers and social researchers claim that people want more than just their own affective happiness: they want happiness originating from the right reasons or standards.

Some social scientists claim that people have a specific need for meaning and purpose, for example Paul Dolan defends a pleasure-purpose-principle: people can be happy through doing pleasant things or through doing things with some purpose.[1] The OECD even accepts the experience of purpose and meaning as a specific type of happiness. We may repeat that, even if meaning and purpose are important conditions for happiness, it is still premature and very inconvenient to include them in the definition, or to discern happiness associated with meaning and purpose as a specific type of happiness.[2]

Combinations of standards can constitute a frame of reference to be applied in the appreciation of specific domains of life, like income, religion, politics, health-care, education and social relations. People may also have ideas about a perfect life, or a perfect world, for example some paradise, utopia, eudaimonia or a classless society without any inequality. They may have such ideas knowingly or unknowingly, but such ideas always have an impact on their cognitive happiness. It may also have a negative impact on their affective happiness, if they feel that there are substantial

[1] Dolan, P. (2014). Happiness by Design. Penguin Group, New York.

[2] There is also a statistical argument: happiness by purpose, as measured by the British Office of National Statistics (ONS), does not represent a separate factor, but is closely related to one and the same evaluative factor. See Kapteyn, A. et al. Dimensions of subjective well-being. Social Indicators Research. September 2015, Volume 123, nr. 3, pp. 625–660.

gaps between the world as it is and how it should be according to their standards.[3]

The normative standards people adopt and apply can be inconsistent with alternative and perhaps more common standards, or just inconsistent with standards we as observers or researchers prefer. Happiness based on specific standards is not by nature morally acceptable or morally superior to anything else.

## The Adoption and Adaptation of Standards

The standards or values people have adopted are very important for their actual behaviour, for their way of life and for their pursuit of happiness. In most nations people are free, at least up to a point, to adopt standards and values and to change them whenever they want to. Identifying and prioritizing values is a typical human enterprise; as expressed by Knight (1964)[4]:

> Life is at bottom an exploration in the field of values, an attempt to discover values, rather than on basis of knowledge of them to produce and enjoy them to the greatest possible extent. We strive to "know ourselves", to find out our real wants, more than to get what we want.

We may assume that the phrase *real wants* refers to our original innate needs, or to values we have discovered and consciously adopted. We can add that finding purpose and meaning in life depends on some active and autonomous adoption of values. Purpose and meaning do not grow by themselves; they require deliberations, discussion and decisions. Amitai Etzioni has described such a process in the context of social change.[5]

People can adopt and adapt standards knowingly, but usually they do so unknowingly without any substantial reflection or deliberation. They adopt or internalize standards of their parents, their school and their social

[3] Frames of reference can be very explicit and developed, like political or religious ideals of a perfect life or a perfect society; some utopia as described by Thomas More. In his book 'Happiness: a History' (2005) Darrin M. McMahon presents some examples of the ideals of early utopian socialists like Cabet, Owen, Fourier and Saint Simon. But people may also have less explicit t ideas about how things should be in their own life and in society.

[4] Knight, F.H. (1964). Risk, Uncertainty, and Profit. New York, A.M. Kelly.

[5] Etzioni, A. (2018) Happiness is the wrong metric; a liberal communitarian response to populism (dedicated to the moral wrestlers). The George Washington University, Washington, DC, USA.

environment in general. The awareness of their own standards is limited and people usually do not know exactly what standards they apply. One implication is that they do not recognize relevant information that might help them to make the best decisions, for example in choosing a hobby, an education, a job or a partner. This inability, to distinguish between relevant and irrelevant information, may lead to 'cognitive peculiarities'.

## Cognitive Peculiarities

People can make mistakes in many ways in their pursuit of happiness. In this context researchers sometimes use terms like 'fallacies' and 'irrationalities', to indicate that people behave in a way that is inconsistent with their own interests or convictions. It is not unusual, however, that researchers use such terms just to indicate that they themselves are critical about some sorts of behaviour. I will use the more neutral term *peculiarities.*

My assumption is that people usually pursue happiness, but sometimes ignore relevant information, or rely on disputable information. If they do so systematically, in some specific ways, we may say that this is a cognitive peculiarity. The negative impact of cognitive peculiarities on happiness is probably limited, but they may have a serious negative impact if they are enforced by social dynamics. Such situations may lead to the adoption of inconvenient, overambitious or inconsistent standards.

We can identify some cognitive peculiarities with this potential impact. This formulation is based not on any judgement of value, but on the observation that the pursuit of happiness is less effective than it could be. There are some everyday peculiarities that deserve our attention: *memory bias, focusing illusions* and *inadequate theories.* More exceptional peculiarities are *underestimation of future adaptation* and more specific is *underestimation of becoming more or less critical about living conditions.*

## Memory Bias, Focusing Illusion and Inadequate Theories

People should learn from their experiences, but the human memory is selective and people don't learn as much as they could from past experiences. Kahneman (1999)[6] discerns some specific types of memory bias:

[6] Kahneman, D. (1999). Objective happiness, in Kahneman, D; Diener, E.; and Schwartz, N. (eds.). Well-being: The foundation of hedonic psychology. New York: Russell Sage Foundation, pp. 3–25.

people tend to remember in particular the most emotional part and the last part of experiences. The duration of experiences is frequently forgotten.

A more general problem is the 'focusing illusion'.[7] Individual ideas about happiness may lack general validity, because they are too focused on current situations. If specific needs are temporally frustrated, they will get a high priority, also as standards in the appreciation of life, but people may fail to reconsider their priorities if the original problems are solved. In economic terminology: people tend to mix up the current marginal impact and the overall long-term impact on happiness of goods, services and conditions.

People develop theories about the determinants of happiness in general and their own happiness in particular. Such theories can be helpful, but can be misleading if they are wrong or outdated. Incorrect theories should be changed, but it takes time to do so. Too much faith in a popular theory can lead to a tunnel vision by ignoring information that is inconsistent with this theory, even if this information is correct and should be used to reject or amend the theory.

## Underestimation of Future Adaptation in General

As a result of the focusing illusion people usually fail to see that their standards and frames of reference will change in the future. Gilbert (2007)[8] presents some humorous examples of people who overestimate the stability of their current standards and make questionable decisions, for example, in buying a house or a car, or in choosing a job or a partner.

Another consequence of this blindness is that people underestimate their potential adaptation, and worry too much about theoretical adversities, like accidents and illness, and overestimate the impact of pleasant changes, like a promotion or winning a lottery. This lack of awareness can be a complication in dealing with changing situations.

[7] Schkade, D.A. and Kahneman, D. (1998). Does Living in California Make People Happy? A Focusing Illusion in Judgements of Life Satisfaction. Psychological Science, 9; 340–346.

[8] Gilbert, D. (2007). Stumbling on happiness. New York, Vintage Books, Random House.

## Underestimation of Becoming More or Less Critical About Living Conditions

The fact that standards and frames of reference change creates yet another fundamental peculiarity. Such changes may imply that people become more or less critical. People can become more critical if conditions are easy, and less critical if conditions are awkward and difficult. One reason is that people, young people and children in particular, need appropriate challenges to flourish, irrespective of the actual conditions.

If conditions are easy, people become more critical in order to create such challenges. In awkward and difficult conditions, they become less critical, in order to keep the challenges manageable and to avoid panic or overheating. This adaptation of standards is therefore related to the 'cybernetic functions' of affective and cognitive happiness: these functions would be problematic if happiness was permanently at a minimum or maximum level.

Set-point-theory claims that people have their own individual 'set point', not only in affective happiness but also in cognitive happiness, and that changes and events have an impact only for a limited period of time.[9] Eventually people will always return to their original personal level of happiness (Brickman and Campbell 1971[10]; Cummins 2010[11]).

Tversky and Griffin (1991)[12] explain this phenomenon more precisely. They make a distinction between an immediate endowment effect of experiences and a longer-term contrast effect. On the one hand, if people have a pleasant experience, they will enjoy a positive endowment effect immediately. They will also have a negative contrast effect in due course, because

[9] This is formulated differently by Brickman and Campbell: people's expectations are raised by pleasant events and lowered by unpleasant ones. The result is that the gap between one's expectations and one's real life remains about the same; so people are on a hedonic- or expectations-treadmill. Brickman, P.D. and Campbell, D.T. (1971). Hedonic relativism and planning the good society. In M.H. Appley (ed.) Adaptation level theory. Academic, New York.

[10] Brickman, P. and Campbell, D.T. (1971). Hedonic relativism and planning the good society. In M.H. Appley (ed.) Adaptation level theory: A Symposium (pp. 287–302) New York: Academic Press.

[11] Cummins, R.A. (2010). Subjective Wellbeing, Homeostatically Protected Mood and Depression: A Synthesis. Journal of Happiness Studies, Volume 11, issue 1, pp. 1–17.

[12] Tversky, A. and Griffin, D. (1991). Endowment and Contrast in Judgements of Well-being; in Strack, F. Argyle, M. and Schwartz, N. (eds.), Subjective Well-being: An Interdisciplinary Perspective, Oxford; Pergamon, pp. 101–118.

they become more critical and demanding. On the other hand, if they have an unpleasant experience, they will become less critical. Then the immediate endowment is negative and the contrast effect is positive. In theory the contrast effect can overrule the immediate endowment effect.

These theories overestimate the potential impact of adaptation.[13] Headey and Wearing (1992)[14] found that events may have an immediate positive or negative impact on happiness (endowment effect), but that the impact on standards or expectations (contrast effect) is much slower and may even take up to two years to be accomplished. Research by Diener et al. (2006)[15] indicates that powerful events can change someone's level of affective happiness for a long period. Losing a spouse or becoming unemployed may have a permanent negative impact (Lucas et al. 2004[16]).

We may conclude, in a nutshell, that the adaptation of standards after powerful positive or negative events, with permanent consequences on living conditions, is not complete. There is, however, some substantial adaptation, and people can be relatively happy in bad conditions and relatively unhappy in good conditions. The relation between subjective happiness and objective events and living conditions can be somewhat loose. This gives rise to an objection against happiness as a standard of well-being, as argued by Amartya Sen (2010).[17]

[13] Some arguments against the set-point-theory are summarized in the World Happiness Report 2017; Measuring and Understanding Happiness: 1: Average life-evaluations differ significantly and systematically among countries, and these differences are substantially explained by life circumstances. 2: There is evidence of long-standing trends in the life evaluations of sub-populations within the same country, demonstrating that life-evaluations can be changed. 3: There is very strong evidence of continuing influence on well-being from major disabilities and unemployment, among other life events. 4: Studies of migration show migrants to have average levels and distributions of life evaluations that resemble those of other residents of their new countries more than of comparable residents in the countries from which they have emigrated.

[14] Headey, B. and Wearing, A. (1992). Understanding Happiness: A theory of subjective well-being. Melbourne, Australia. Longman Cheshire Pty Limited.

[15] Diener, E., Lucas R., Scollon, C.N. (2006) Beyond the Hedonic Treadmill: Revisiting the adaptation theory of well-being. American Psychologist 61 (4): 305–314.

[16] Lucas, R., Clark, A. E., Georgellis, Y., Diener, E. (2004). Unemployment alters the set-point for life satisfaction. Psychological Science. 15 (1) 8–13.

[17] Sen, A. (2010). The idea of justice. Penguin books. Page 283. "The practical merit of such adjustments for people in chronically adverse positions is easy to understand: this is one way of being able to live peacefully with persistent deprivation. But the adjustments also have the consequential effect of distorting the scale of utilities in he form of happiness or desire-fulfilment."

There is, however, no indication that the impact of objective events and conditions is completely overruled by adaptation. If this were the case then it would be unlikely to find any substantial correlation between happiness and objective living conditions. Empirical research indicates that there is still a substantial correlation and that the impact of adaptation is not unlimited.

An interesting theoretical question in this respect is how much deterioration in living conditions could be managed by adaptation. Would people in rich nations become unhappy in the event of a reduction of consumption, for example, if this was inevitable in order to reduce pollution or to maintain biodiversity? And if they became unhappy, how long would it take to adapt and to get back to their original happiness level? Hopefully it will never be required, but we may expect some substantial adaptation as long as fundamental needs, related to physical and social safety, are gratified.

## Peculiarities and Social Dynamics

The peculiarities mentioned above have some negative impact on the short-term pursuit of happiness, but this negative impact is not necessarily very substantial in the long term. Happiness receives a lot of critical attention, and inadequate ideas and theories can be repaired by research, education, discussion and 'management by speech'. Some peculiarities are probably inevitable, and perhaps even amusing. The key problem is, however, that the long-term negative impact can become substantial through the role of social dynamics. We have to be critical about social dynamics like *social comparison*, *positional competition*, *secondary inflation* and *manipulation*.

## Social Dynamics: Social Comparison

Standards, frames of reference and preferences can be changed by social comparison. Social comparison can be informative and inspiring, if people observe, for example, how other people live and make a living. It can also have a negative impact on happiness, if it makes people adopt unreasonable or unrealistic standards. Social comparison can have a very negative impact if there is a high level of unjustifiable inequality and conspicuous consumption. In such conditions social comparison can easily contribute to feelings of insecurity, anxiety and frustration. Wilkinson, Stiglitz and

Graham have published some important research findings about this phenomenon.[18] Commercial organizations can provoke and manipulate social comparison deliberately, to make people buy specific commodities or services.

## Social Dynamics: Positional Competition

Many people try to improve their individual or household position in terms of income, wealth and status. This is understandable for several reasons. One reason is that a low social-economic status has a negative impact on happiness. This negative impact can be reduced by effective social security.[19,20] Higher relative positions also create more safety and security, irrespective of the absolute level of wealth and income. People in higher positions have more information, less stress and are less vulnerable to adversity. Having a relatively high amount of money makes it easier to move to a better neighbourhood if needed, and to organize medical and personal care in case of serious health problems. This is particularly important in nations without adequate public provisions and services. In such nations people must always put a high priority on money, even if they are already well-off, and not materialistic by nature.

In many societies such priorities and efforts contribute to more productivity and happiness, but in rich nations this effect is less pronounced, because labour productivity is high already. People can still improve their individual position, but this will go together with a deterioration in the relative position of other people. Average income and wealth can still go up in a nominal way, but not substantially in terms of real purchasing power. In such situations individual efforts to improve individual positions are ineffective on balance. This is a zero-sum situation in terms of well-being and happiness.

[18] Wilkinson, R.. (2005). The impact of inequality: how to make sick societies healthier. Routledge; London; Stiglitz, J. (2012). The price of inequality. W.W. Norton & Company. New York; Graham, C. (2017). Happiness for all? Princeton University Press. New Jersey.

[19] See Samuel, R, and Hadjar, A. (2016). How welfare-state regimes shape subjective well-being across Europe. Social Indicators Research, nr. 129: pp. 565–587.

[20] Hochrat, O. and Skopek, N. (2013). The impact of wealth on subjective well-being: A comparison of three welfare-state regimes. Research in Social Stratification and Mobility 34: 127–141. Inequality in household wealth has no impact on subjective well-being (happiness) due to efficient social security.

Organizing personal safety and security at an individual level is very cost-ineffective in rich nations. We may carefully conclude that there is a certain risk that people in rich nations will get stuck in a rat-race without proportional benefits. This may even happen if people do not want to improve their own relative position ('surpass the Joneses'), but just want to protect their own relative position ('keeping up with the Joneses') (Lichtenberg 1996).[21] Commercial, religious and political organizations can activate people and provoke such a rat-race for their own interests.

## Social Dynamics: Secondary Inflation

According to Hirata (2003),[22] "…secondary inflation takes place to the degree that structural social changes reduce the rate at which a given good can be transformed into functioning, or equivalently, to the degree that the costs of a given functioning in terms of inputs increase." Just as (primary) inflation means an increase of money units required per good, so secondary inflation means an increase in the amount of real resources required per functioning. Hirata adds, following Sen (1985)[23]: "The concept of functioning refers to the things a person can actually do with a particular good, what a person 'manages to do or to be'".

Layard (1980)[24] presents a nice example of secondary inflation: "…in a poor society a man proves to his wife that he loves her by giving her a rose but in a rich society he must give her a dozen roses." In rich nations commodities and events with some symbolic connotation, like presents, fashion and parties, have to be expensive to get the required meaning or importance. Marketing people obviously use such rules of 'symbolic interactionism' to stimulate people to spend more money. It would be nice if

[21] Lichtenberg, J. (1996). Consuming because others consume. Social Theory & Practice, 22(3): 273–297.

[22] Hirata, J. (2011). Happiness, Ethics and Economics. Routledge, Taylor & Francis Group, London and New York, page 46. The term 'secondary inflation' was first introduced in Hirata, J. (2001): Happiness and Economics: Enriching Economic Theory with Empirical Psychology, Master's thesis, Maastricht University, page 36. The term was first published in Vendrik, M. and Hirata, J. (2003). Experienced versus Decision Utility of Income: Relative or Absolute Happiness, in Bruni, L. and Porta, P.L. (eds.), Handbook of the Economics of Happiness, Cheltenham: Edward Elgar, pp. 185–208.

[23] Sen, A. (1985). Commodities and Capabilities. Professor Dr. P. Hennipman Lectures in Economics. Amsterdam, North-Holland.

[24] Layard, R. (1980). Human satisfaction and public policy. The Economic Journal, 90(360): 737–750.

people could agree that one rose is really enough, and if parents could agree that expensive clothes and parties are not needed for their children, but it is difficult to reach such agreements. This is a typical prisoner's dilemma.

How serious is this problem? This is a difficult question. But we have to pay attention to the fact that many Dutch florists have invested money in some poor African nations, like Kenya and Ethiopia, to grow roses; even though this creates serious local problems or negative external effects, in the terminology of economists. There are pollution and a shortage of clean water. Similar stories can be told about golf-courses, textile production and casinos in poor nations. Key point is that the gratification of marginal needs of rich people goes together with some serious frustration of the fundamental needs of poor people. We may speculate that both Mandeville and Smith would disqualify such activities as imprudent and immoral. Perhaps Mandeville would advocate an intervention by some national or supranational government in the context of a more comprehensive development strategy. Smith would probably prefer to rely on the impact of the invisible hand of free markets to improve this situation in due time.

It might be a step in the right direction to agree that the need for clean water is more fundamental than the need for flowers, because clean water is a prerequisite for physical safety and for the gratification of other needs, while the need for flowers is less fundamental in this respect. If there is some consensus on this point, it might be an option to organize the markets in such a way that the gratification of fundamental needs gets a higher priority.

## Social Dynamics: Manipulation

Standards, frames of reference and preferences are heavily manipulated. People all over the world are continuously bombarded with commercials to make them spend more money and buy more goods and services. Usually such commercials try to suggest that there are serious gaps between *life as it is* and *life as it could and should be* in the perceptions of potential consumers. But standards and frames of reference, and preferences or wants, are also manipulated by employers, friends, partners and politicians, who all have their own interests.

This manipulation can have a negative impact on happiness, if people are frustrated in identifying and dealing with their own original needs and standards.[25] Manipulation makes people too restless, too demanding and too critical about their living conditions. People can become 'utility monsters'[26] or 'miserable misers'. Manipulation may even contribute to pollution and the exhaustion of resources, without any benefits in happiness or objective well-being. Financial dependency and insecurity facilitate manipulation.

## The Negative Impact of Positional Competition on the Pursuit of Happiness

The inventory of some—certainly not all—peculiarities and social dynamics is also interesting because knowledge can help us to pursue happiness more effectively, if we decide to do so. All peculiarities and dynamics are, in a way, normal aspects of human interaction. The peculiarities have by definition some short-term negative impact on happiness, but up to a point this is inevitable and not very serious. Social dynamics are also normal aspects of human interaction and none of them is negative by definition. Even manipulation can be beneficial and justifiable.

The problem is that the peculiarities and dynamics hang together and can go wrong together. Positional competition is a key issue in this respect. Positional competition contributes to happiness and objective well-being if there is some scarcity, as explained by Adam Smith. Efforts invested in positional competition go together with substantial benefits in production and consumption. Such benefits may compensate for the negative consequences of competition, like financial insecurity and stress.

The situation is very different once high levels of technology, productivity and prosperity have been reached. In this new situation the benefits of efforts invested in positional competition are relatively low and cannot compensate for the negative consequences.

[25] An interesting concept in this context is "psychological freedom" as defined by Christian Bay: the degree of harmony between basic motives and overt behaviour; in Bay, C. (1958). The structure of freedom. Stanford, CA: Stanford University Press. Manipulation has a very negative impact on this type of freedom.

[26] Nozick, Robert (1974). Anarchy, State, and Utopia. p. 41. Another 'thought experiment' as a critical comment on utilitarianism: if anyone would enjoy unlimited utility from one unit of resources, he or she should get all available resources, because this would create the greatest utility or happiness. We have to keep in mind, however, that only utility can be unlimited; happiness is limited by nature.

If we maintain positional competition in this situation, we may indeed expect that the dynamics of social comparison, secondary inflation and manipulation, and of peculiarities like focusing illusion, adaptation and inadequate theories, will be used as instruments in this competition. The negative impact of social dynamics and cognitive peculiarities will become more substantial due to the impact of positional competition.

If we want more happiness, we should try to minimize the necessity of positional competition.[27] One way to do it is the introduction of a basic income. For many people a basic income will be insufficient, but for some people it will be enough, and then they will have some freedom to avoid positional competition.[28]

An alternative and perhaps better way is to reduce the negative impact of a low income, by organizing adequate public goods. The Scandinavian countries are very successful in this respect, by making sure that important provisions, like medical care and education, are available for everybody irrespective of income. This is also a way to protect children against the negative impact of poverty of their parents.

There is, according to Headey and Wearing (1992),[29] no justification for pessimism about the impact of positional competition. In their view positional competition can play a role in the domains of *work and material standard of living*, but not in the other five domains of life. At this point they formulate an optimistic proposition (nr. 3.3):

> At least five of the (seven) priority domains—marriage and sex, friendship and leisure, and health—are characterised by non-zero sum satisfactions. In these domains everyday pleasures and satisfactions can be obtained while enhancing and not subtracting from other people's pleasures and satisfactions. This makes it possible for most people to attain a high level of well-being.

The last sentence is clearly too optimistic, because *work and material standard of living* are crucial for personal development and social and financial security. Positional competition in these domains can have a very negative impact on happiness.

[27] Ott, J. (2011). How much competition do we need in a civilized society? Journal of Happiness Studies, 12(3), 525–529. Review of the book 'Winning: Reflections on an American Obsession (2011) by Francesco Duina; Princeton and Oxford. University Press.

[28] A negative income tax, as formulated by M. Friedman, is an interesting alternative, but requires more supervision to avoid abuse. See: Friedman, M. Capitalism and Freedom (1962). University of Chicago Press.

[29] Headey, B. and Wearing, A. (1992). Understanding Happiness: A theory of subjective well-being. Melbourne, Australia. Longman Cheshire Pty Limited.

## Consistency, Comparability and Stability of Cognitive Happiness?

We will consider the consistency and comparability of overall happiness in the next chapters, but here we will briefly consider the consistency, comparability and stability of cognitive happiness. People are free to adopt and adapt their standards at will. Theoretically they may adopt inconsistent and very different standards and change them frequently. This would be a serious problem for the consistency, comparability and stability of cognitive happiness. There are, however, good reasons to believe that people adopt consistent and similar standards, and do not change them in some unpredictable or volatile way.

(a) About consistency: people pursue consistency in their selection of standards because it is very practical and convenient to have a consistent appreciation of life. A consistent appreciation facilitates quick and adequate decisions in view of new opportunities and problems. It is also beneficial for people's peace of mind.
(b) Most people respect the importance of the gratification of general human needs as a standard. Some values and living conditions are therefore appreciated by most people, like minimal respect, respect for human rights, security, health-care, social relations and the availability of food. Such conditions play a crucial role for well-being in objective list theories.[30]
(c) Standards and frames of reference become more universal by convergence, as a consequence of globalization and international communication. Non-commercial international organizations, like the United Nations and the International Labour Organization, play an important role in this respect, for example in the formulation and protection of human rights (*standard-setting*).
(d) An additional cause of convergence is commercial advertising which exploits social dynamics like social comparison, positional competition, secondary inflation and manipulation. People are encouraged to spend more and more money for the same commodities and services, for example for conspicuous consumption in terms of appearances and lifestyles. The impact on the pursuit of

[30] Rice, C. (2013). Defending the Objective List Theory of Well-Being. Ratio, An international journal of analytic philosophy; Vol. 26, Issue 2, pp. 196–211. Wiley & Sons Ltd.

happiness is negative, but it contributes to the convergence of standards.

(e) Standards and frames of reference are basic and stable elements in cultures and they usually do not change overnight. The impact of changes in standards on the longitudinal comparability of happiness is limited. This will be different if there are dramatic changes in the social-economic environment.

(f) Standards and frames of reference can change in the same way for different individuals or groups. In such situations the impact on the interpersonal comparability of happiness is limited, even if the longitudinal comparability is reduced.

## The Next Steps

The observations related to affective and cognitive happiness are interesting. There are indeed good reasons to believe that both affective and cognitive happiness have some internal consistency and some interpersonal and longitudinal comparability. These arguments seem to be somewhat more convincing for affective than for cognitive happiness. Individual freedom has, at least theoretically, more impact on cognitive happiness than on affective happiness. This expectation deserves more attention, in order to predict the results of the interaction between affective and cognitive happiness. Chapters 5 and 6 are about the consistency and comparability of overall happiness.

## Bibliography

Brickman, P., & Campbell, D. T. (1971). Hedonic relativism and planning the good society. In M. H. Appley (Ed.), *Adaptation level theory: A symposium* (pp. 287–302). New York: Academic Press.

Cummins, R. A. (2010). Subjective wellbeing, homeostatically protected mood and depression: A synthesis. *Journal of Happiness Studies, 11*(1), 1–17.

Diener, E., Lucas, R., & Scollon, C. N. (2006). Beyond the hedonic treadmill: Revisiting the adaptation theory of well-being. *American Psychologist, 61*(4), 305–314.

Gilbert, D. (2007). *Stumbling on happiness.* New York: Vintage Books, Random House.

Headey, B., & Wearing, A. (1992). *Understanding happiness: A theory of subjective well-being*. Melbourne: Longman Cheshire Pty Limited.

Kahneman, D. (1999). Objective happiness. In D. Kahneman, E. Diener, & N. Schwartz (Eds.), *Well-being: The foundation of hedonic psychology* (pp. 3–25). New York: Russell Sage Foundation.

Knight, F. H. (1964). *Risk, uncertainty, and profit*. New York: A.M. Kelly.

Layard, R. (1980). Human satisfaction and public policy. *The Economic Journal, 90*(360), 737–750.

Lichtenberg, J. (1996). Consuming because others consume. *Social Theory & Practice, 22*(3), 273–297.

Lucas, R., Clark, A. E., Georgellis, Y., & Diener, E. (2004). Unemployment alters the set-point for life satisfaction. *Psychological Science, 15*(1), 8–13.

Sen, A. (1985). *Commodities and capabilities*. Professor Dr. P. Hennipman Lectures in Economics. Amsterdam, North Holland.

Sen, A. (2010). *The idea of justice*. London: Penguin books.

Tversky, A., & Griffin, D. (1991). Endowment and contrast in judgements of well-being. In F. Strack, M. Argyle, & N. Schwartz (Eds.), *Subjective well-being: An interdisciplinary perspective* (pp. 101–118). Oxford: Pergamon.

CHAPTER 5

# Back to Overall Happiness: It Exists!

## Discussions About the Body and the Mind as Origins of Affective and Cognitive Happiness

There has been, and still is, discussion about the relative importance of affective and cognitive happiness. There are some similarities between this discussion and philosophical discussions about the importance of the body and the mind.

Affective happiness, with emotions and moods as elements, is sometimes supposed to be related to the material-biological body. This body can be understood and explained in terms of general causal relations. The role of individual freedom is limited in this type of happiness. Cognitive happiness, with thoughts and judgements as elements, is occasionally supposed to be related to the spiritual mind. The usual assumption is that this mind is free, and therefore not subject to explanations in terms of causal relations.[1] The role of individual freedom is substantial in cognitive happiness, because people can adopt or reject standards at will. They can even

[1] As nicely expressed in the German Song: "Die Gedanken sind Frei" (thoughts are free) with this first strophe:

Thoughts are free, who can guess them?
They fly by like nocturnal shadows.
No person can know them, no hunter can shoot them
with powder and lead: Thoughts are free!


J. Ott, *Beyond Economics*,
https://doi.org/10.1007/978-3-030-56600-5_5

decide to put a high or a low priority on their hedonic experience of positive and negative emotions, relative to their priorities for anything else, like becoming a famous pianist or football player.

The discussion about the importance of the body and the mind is obviously not quite the same as the discussion about affective and cognitive happiness. Affective happiness depends a great deal on the gratification of biological needs, but also on perceived gaps between 'is' and 'ought'. The similarity between cognitive happiness and the mind is even more debatable.

Human cognition and cognitive happiness can be defined rather precisely, while the concept of ***mind*** is difficult. As formulated by Gilbert Ryle (1949), "The mind is everything non-somatic: a sort of a ghost in the machine", and: "Mind is a philosophical illusion hailing chiefly from Rene Descartes and sustained by logical errors and 'category mistakes' which have become habitual."[2]

It is correct, however, that the body and affective happiness are characterized by a relatively low level of individual freedom, while the spiritual mind and cognitive happiness are characterized by a relatively high level of individual freedom. Putting priority on biology and affective happiness is therefore related to a materialistic and deterministic vision of human reality. Putting priority on the mind and cognitive happiness is related to a hermeneutic vision with more indeterminacy, focusing on freedom, meaning, interpretation and arguments. It is therefore interesting and informative to pay attention to discussions about the body, as the origin of affective happiness, and the mind, as the origin of cognitive happiness.

In 1641 Descartes published his *Meditations*[3] with his theory of the dualism of the body and the mind, made of different substances and with the pineal gland as the connection between the two. He also found that his cognition, or thinking, was the ultimate proof of his existence ('cogito ergo sum'[4]). The implication is that the body and the mind are different realities, but that the mind is steering the body.

[2] Ryle, G. (1949) The concept of mind. University of Chicago Press (edition 2002). The work has been cited as having "put the final nail in the coffin of Cartesian dualism".

[3] Descartes. (1641). Meditationes de prima philosophia.

[4] Descartes (1644). Principia philosophiae.

In 1748 Julien Offray de La Mettrie published his *L'Homme Machine*, with his opposite and outspoken materialistic vision that the mind is subordinated to the body.[5] In 1789 Bentham published his *Principles of Morals and Legislation*, starting with these sentences:

> Nature has placed mankind under the governance of two sovereign masters, *pain* and *pleasure*. It is for them alone to point out what we ought to do, as well as to determine what we shall do.[6]

Bentham is not explicit about the body and the mind, but these sentences suggest that in his view the material affective component is the dominant component in happiness. The views of de la Mettrie and Bentham are supported by Damasio, who published his *Descartes' Error, Emotions, Reason and the Human Brain* in 1994.[7] He presents empirical evidence showing that the emotions are dominant. People can live without cognition, but not without emotions. Without emotions they get stuck in some paralysing indifference, and then they are unable to make decisions or to evaluate anything, let alone their life as a whole. Perhaps this is understandable since most emotions and moods are experienced as *positive or negative*, while this is more debatable for thoughts. This vision, about the supremacy of emotions, is supported by Zajonc (1980, 1984[8]), Veenhoven (2009[9]), Kainulainen and Veenhoven (2015[10]). If people are faced with

[5] Julien Offray de La Mettrie (1748). L'Homme Machine (1748).

[6] Bentham, J. (1789). The Principles of Morals and Legislation; first Chapter, first sentence. With an interesting footnote about the concepts of utility, happiness and felicity.

[7] Damasio, A. (1994). Descartes' Error, Emotions, Reason and the Human Brain. Harper Perennial.

[8] Zajonc, R.B., (1980). Feelings and Thinking: Preferences Need No Inferences. American Psychologist, 35: 151–175. And (1984) On the primacy of affect. American Psychologist, 39 (2) 117–123.

[9] Veenhoven, R. (2009) *How do we assess how happy we are?* Tenets, implications and tenability of three theories'. Ii: Dutt, A. K. & Radcliff, B. (eds.) 'Happiness, Economics and Politics: Towards a multi-disciplinary approach', Edward Elger Publishers, Cheltenham UK, Chapter 3, page 45–69.

[10] Kainulainen, S. and Veenhoven R. (2018). Life-Satisfaction is more a matter of feeling-well than having -what-you-want. International Journal of Happiness and Development, vol. 4, nr. 3, pp. 209–235

dilemmas in their appreciation of life, or if they want to buy some flowers, they will use their affect as a referee. *Hedonist theories* of happiness put priority on affective happiness, as the balance of enjoyment and suffering.

Some philosophers and researchers, on the other hand, are critical about such statements. They do not reject the importance of affective happiness, but claim that cognition plays a crucial role. Such visions are expressed in *informed desire theories*, with some knowledge as a condition,[11] in *authentic happiness theories* with an affective and cognitive component as necessary conditions,[12] and in *Aristotelian theories* with an accent on the importance of virtue.

We may add that people want consistent theories about the world and their personal position and happiness. Such theories are convenient because they facilitate personal decisions. If they have incompatible criteria, or if their criteria are too demanding, they will get frustrated and unhappy. So they can become unhappy due to some awkward cognitive evaluation. They can also make themselves feel better by cognitive exercises, like expressing gratitude to somebody or counting their blessings. Some behavioural therapists recommend such exercises. It is also interesting, in this context, that placebo pills, without any active components, can have a substantial positive impact on human emotions. This impact is even observable on MRI-scans of the brains.

The arguments in favour of affect and feelings are somewhat more convincing than the arguments in favour of cognition and thoughts, but the final proof is still missing, and perhaps we will never see it. The best and most practical solution, at least for the time being, is to accept that the rather philosophical discussion about any dominance, of either the mind or the body, is undecided. Perhaps that is because it is simply incorrect to assume that the body and the mind are different realities. Perhaps it is more realistic to assume that the body is a pre-condition for sensorial experience, emotions, perception and thinking, as defended by Merleau-Ponty (1945).[13] In this vision the interaction between affective and cognitive happiness is not based on dominance of either one, but on parity and mutual dependence. At this point we may add that affective happiness is based on actual experiences, and is sometimes denoted as *experiential*

[11] Griffin, J. (1986) Well-being: its meaning, measurement, and moral importance. Clarendon, Oxford.

[12] Sumner, L.W. (1996) Welfare, Happiness, and Ethics. New York, Oxford University Press.

[13] Merleau-Ponty, M. (1945). Phénoménologie de la perception. Gallimard, Paris.

*happiness*, while cognitive happiness is based on some reflection, about such experiences or anything else, and is sometimes denoted as *evaluative happiness*.

This is an interesting compromise, but we still have to deal with the questions mentioned in the previous chapters, but now without any expectations about dominance: are affective and cognitive happiness in general consistent? Or more practically: are they usually at the same or similar levels? We may only use the phrase 'overall happiness', or 'happiness in general', or 'encompassing happiness', if there is at least some minimal consistency. We must distinguish between short- and long-term affective happiness to assess the consistency with cognitive happiness.

## The Distinction Between Short- and Long-Term Affective Happiness

Short-term affective happiness is about momentary emotions or emotions during short periods of time such as a day or a week.[14] Long-term affective happiness is about average emotions over longer periods. This is simple, but we have to keep in mind that there are more fluctuations in short-term affective happiness, and with different determinants, than in long-term affective happiness. It is like the weather: we have our daily weather and we have our long-term climate. This metaphor is perhaps not perfect in every respect, since our climate is changing while our long-term affective happiness is relatively stable.

The stability of long-term affective happiness depends on enduring emotional dispositions, like cheerfulness and pessimism. Such dispositions depend on their turns on the current and past gratification of needs, but also on factors like emotional experiences, personality and genes. Some people are always cheerful and optimistic, almost irrespective of their living conditions and personal history. There are also people who are always gloomy and pessimistic, irrespective of anything. Such stability, however, is exceptional; most people experience substantial fluctuations in their short-term affective happiness, while their long-term affective happiness is relatively stable, due to their more permanent emotional dispositions.

[14] We leave moods out of consideration for shortness.

## Short-Term Affective Happiness: Two Reasons to Expect Inconsistency with Cognitive Happiness

- One trivial reason to expect inconsistency is that there are frequent fluctuations in short-term affective happiness, while cognitive happiness is rather stable. Our emotions can be very negative at specific moments or for relatively short periods of time, for example due to some physical condition like illness, a hangover or some unpleasant event, while our cognitive evaluation of life is positive. It can also be the other way around: people can feel good, even if they know they are not successful in some other respects.
- Emotions in the past, for example in childhood, can have an impact on current affective happiness. Negative or positive emotions can 'pop up' unexpectedly, if they are triggered by specific conditions or events.

## Short-Term Affective Happiness: One Reason to Expect Consistency with Cognitive Happiness

- Even without interaction we may expect some consistency: pleasant events and conditions provoke pleasant emotions and positive thoughts, and unpleasant events and conditions provoke unpleasant emotions and negative thoughts.

## Long-Term Affective Happiness: One Reason to Expect Inconsistency with Cognitive Happiness

- People are free to adopt whatever standards they prefer to evaluate their life. They can even adopt standards that are inimical to emotional well-being, for example, if they are very ambitious and want to do something special, for example win some gold medals at the Olympics, become a famous pianist or die as a martyr. There is no inconsistency if they succeed and feel good, or if they fail and feel miserable, but there can be inconsistency if they succeed but feel miserable, or if they fail but feel good.

## Long-Term Affective Happiness: Four Reasons to Expect Consistency with Cognitive Happiness

- People tend to adopt affective happiness as a standard, even if they do so with different priorities. Some minimum emotional well-being is needed as a precondition for anything else.
- The adoption of many standards is not emotionally neutral; the adoption of standards like solidarity and justice has a positive emotional connotation.
- More fundamental are the long-term interaction effects: positive emotions in childhood facilitate cognitive development,[15] and cognitive attitudes and dispositions, once they are established, will discourage or facilitate specific emotions.[16] An interesting finding in this context is that the mental health of the mother is an important factor for the future happiness of her children.[17] This is an important observation, because the implication is that affective happiness in the past has a substantial impact on current and future happiness. We might underestimate this impact if we just look at current conditions.
- People think a lot about their life as a whole and try to develop some consistent evaluation of it, also in terms of affect and cognition. They can be creative in this evaluation. If their emotional well-being is bad, while they are successful in other ways, they can be inclined to put a low priority on affective happiness and a high priority on cognitive happiness. It can go the other way around, if they are unhappy about their personal position and achievements, but feel good for different reasons. In both ways they can conclude that their overall happiness is positive. Perhaps the first strategy is attractive for older people who feel less energetic, but can look back with contentment

[15] Frederickson, B.L. (2001). The role of positive emotions in positive psychology: The Broaden-and-Build theory of Positive Emotions. American Psychologist, 56 (3), 218-226.

[16] Conway, A. (2013) et al. The Broaden-and-Build theory of Positive Emotions: Form, Function, and Mechanisms. In: The Oxford Handbook of Happiness. David, S., Boniwell, I., and Conley Ayers, A. eds. Oxford University Press.

[17] Clark, A. et al. (2018). The Origins of Happiness. Princeton University Press. Princeton & Oxford.

at their achievements. The second strategy is perhaps more appropriate for young people because their achievements are still 'under construction'. In a nutshell: people can be flexible, and put the highest priority on the most successful component, to create some pleasant consistency.

## Conclusion About Consistency: Good Enough; Overall Happiness Is a Reality

If we compare the theoretical reasons to expect consistency or inconsistency between affective and cognitive happiness, we may argue that the consistency is questionable for short-term happiness. This conclusion is supported by the modest correlation between the frequencies of positive or negative emotions and cognitive happiness during specific periods.[18]

The reasons to expect consistency between long-term affective and cognitive happiness are convincing. The support from social-psychological research, about the cumulative impact of positive emotions on emotional and cognitive development, is clear. This conclusion is supported by the fact that people find it easy to answer questions about their overall happiness. It is difficult, however, to measure long-term affective happiness with simple questions in a questionnaire. As a consequence there is a lack of information about long-term happiness, and about the relations between long-term affective happiness and cognitive happiness.

The conclusion here is, nevertheless, that we may expect consistency, because of the convincing theoretical reasons discussed above. We may therefore assume that there is indeed such a thing as overall happiness, defined as the appreciation of life as a whole. Perhaps we may speculate that overall happiness is a phenomenon with two anchors: long-term affective happiness may have some moderating impact on the adoption of

[18] See Chap. 6. Pearson r is usually around 0.4 if an Affect Balance Scale is used, but lower for frequencies of negative emotions and higher for frequencies of positive emotions. The correlation between average cognitive happiness in nations and average frequencies of negative emotions is -0.29, while this correlation is +0.54 for average frequencies of positive emotions (Gallup World Poll 2012–2019). We see similar correlations at an individual level within nations.

new standards, while cognitive happiness may have some moderating impact on emotional fluctuations. The anchors are attached to elastic cables; they create some stability but leave room for flexibility. In the next chapter the comparability of happiness will be assessed using more results from empirical research.

## Bibliography

de La Mettrie, J. O. (1748). *L'Homme Machine.*

Merleau-Ponty, M. (1945). *Phénoménologie de la perception.* Paris: Gallimard.

Ryle, G. (1949). *The concept of mind.* Chicago, IL: University of Chicago Press. (edition 2002).

Zajonc, R. (1984). On the primacy of affect. *American Psychologist, 39*(2), 117–123.

CHAPTER 6

# The Measurement and Explanation of Happiness

## The World Database of Happiness

In many nations there are regular surveys[1] with questions about affective happiness, with positive and negative emotions as elements, cognitive and overall happiness. The World Database of Happiness (WDH) at the University of Rotterdam[2] contains a lot of information about happiness research, including information about approximately 1400 different measures to measure happiness, mostly single questions (in August 2020). This diversity is related to some important differences in survey questions.

(a) Differences in focus: directed at affective happiness (code A), cognitive happiness (code C of contentment) or overall happiness (code O)
(b) Differences in time frames: now, last moment, last day, currently/today/presently, or last week, month, last weeks, quarter, year
(c) Differences in observation method: single or multiple questions, open or projective questioning, focused interview, ratings by family, nurses, peers, teachers, interviewers

[1] Like the World Values Surveys, surveys by Gallup, the General Social Surveys in the US, the British Household Panel, The German Social Economic Panel.

[2] Veenhoven, R., *World Database of Happiness*, Erasmus University Rotterdam, The Netherlands. http://worlddatabaseofhappiness.eur.nl. Some additional information about the collections (August 2020): 14746 publications in Bibliography of happiness; 17331 distributional findings and 19871 correlational findings.


J. Ott, *Beyond Economics*,
https://doi.org/10.1007/978-3-030-56600-5_6

(d) Differences in ratings by verbal, numerical or graphical scales, with different range, for example 1–7 or 1–10

It is obviously problematic to compare the answers, if different happiness questions have been asked. It is informative to pay attention to the differences in focus on either affective, cognitive or overall happiness.

### *The Measurement of Affective Happiness*

Affective happiness consists of emotions.[3] The key point in measuring affective happiness is that people are invited to report about their positive and negative emotions during a specific period or at specific moments. They are supposed to do so spontaneously, without too much reflection. The usual assumption is that frequencies of negative and positive emotions are an expression of the appreciation or enjoyment of life as a whole. There are three well-known approaches to asking questions about affective happiness.

In the first approach people are invited to make an inventory of specific positive and negative emotions in a specific period, for example the previous day or week. The difference in the frequencies of positive and negative emotions can be interpreted as an Affect-Balance Scale (ABS). There are many ways to make an Affect Balance Scale, by selecting and defining different positive and negative emotions.[4] It is also possible to count and assess positive and negative emotions as independent indicators, without paying attention to the balance between them.

A second approach is the Day-Reconstruction Method as developed by Kahneman et al. (2004).[5] People are invited to make an inventory of their actual activities on the previous day, and to assess their emotions during these activities.

A third approach is the Experience Sampling Methods as developed by Csikzentmihalyi and Hunter (2003).[6] People are invited to report their

[3] We leave moods out of consideration for shortness.

[4] One example: the Affect Balance Scale developed by Bradburn. Bradburn N.M.(1969). *The structure of psychological well-being*. Chicago: Aldine.

[5] Kahneman, D., Kreuger, A. B., & Schkade, D. A. (2004). A survey method for characterizing daily life experience: The day reconstruction method. Science, 306, 1776–1780.

[6] Csikzentmihalyi, M., & Hunter, J. (2003). The use of experience sampling. Journal of Happiness Studies, 4(2), 185–199.

actual emotions and moods several times a day, at random moments, usually using their mobile phone. An important advantage of this approach is that people can also report about their less clear-cut moods; the first and second approaches are usually about emotions, because memorizing moods is less reliable.

### *Problems in Measuring Affective Happiness*

Measuring affective happiness through positive and negative emotions is difficult. There are regular and irregular fluctuations in emotions and moods. Many observations are needed to get an impression of such fluctuations and the underlying trends. Another problem is that our memory is limited and perhaps selective. The acceptability of emotions may have an impact on our memory. The intensity of emotions is usually neglected, probably because it is even more complicated to measure intensity than frequencies. This is unfortunate because mild positive and negative emotions can go together, while this is less likely for intensive positive and negative emotions.

These measurement problems are rather technical, but an underlying fundamental problem is that positive and negative emotions have different dynamics. The frequencies of positive emotions are higher than the frequencies of negative emotions. Positive emotions are a condition for cognitive and emotional development.[7] Negative emotions can be an obstacle in this respect. They are related to the frustration of fundamental needs, like the need for safety and security. They can be related to dangerous or unpleasant events or situations, and can have an enduring negative impact on emotional and cognitive development, and on overall happiness in due course.

We may conclude that it is difficult to measure affective happiness over longer periods. There are options for improvement. It would be better to measure emotions more often and over longer periods, with more attention to the intensity. It is also important to measure emotions in childhood, because they are important for emotional and cognitive development. It would be helpful, furthermore, to collect some information about

[7] Frederickson, B.L. (2001). The role of positive emotions in positive psychology: The broaden-and-build theory of positive emotions. American Psychologist, 56 (3), 218–226.

personality and the occurrence of mental problems. It is obviously difficult to collect such personal and complex information systematically, with simple survey questions.[8] Panel studies, where the same people are followed over longer periods, also in childhood, are more appropriate.

### *The Measurement of Cognitive Happiness*

The key point in measuring the cognitive component, sometimes denoted as contentment, is that people are invited to think first, for example, about their life and their personal situation, before they answer a question. A well-known example is the so-called ladder scale as developed by Cantril (1965).[9]

> The question is: 'Please imagine a ladder, with steps numbered from 0 at the bottom to 10 at the top. The top of the ladder represents the best possible life for you and the bottom of the ladder represents the worst possible life for you. On which step of the ladder would you say you personally feel you stand at this time?'
>
> 0 1 2 3 4 5 6 7 8 9 10
> *Bottom of the ladder* *Top of the ladder*

This survey question, or the 'life ladder', is used in the Gallup World Poll in many nations. The scale is qualified as a 'self-anchoring scale' since the respondents are free to determine the upper and lower limits of the scale in accordance with their own experiences or imaginations. If people have some frame of reference about the best and the worst possible life, then we may assume that such frames of reference will determine their upper and lower limit. According to some researchers a 'self-anchoring scale' will not produce very different answers compared to other scales, because people will use their imagination anyway, whether they are invited to do so or not.[10]

[8] Information about mental problems might also contribute to a better epidemiological understanding of types of mental illness, like depression and anxiety. Mental illness has a negative impact on happiness; see also: Layard, R. (2018). Mental illness destroys happiness and is costless to treat. In J. Sachs (Ed.), Global Happiness: Policy Report 2018, 27–52. New York: Sustainable Development Solutions Network.

[9] Cantril, H. (1965). The pattern of human concerns. New York, NY: New Brunswick.

[10] Lefcowits, M.J. and Wallston, B. (1973). Self-Anchoring Scale: Does it make a difference? Sociological Methods & Research, Volume 1, issue 3, pages 387–399. Sage Publications.

### *Problems in Measuring Cognitive Happiness*

The measurement of cognitive happiness is easier than measuring affective happiness, because people think a lot about their life and there is more stability. It is, however, problematic to measure the cognitive happiness of young people and children, since their cognitive happiness is still 'under construction'. It is also problematic, obviously, to measure the cognitive happiness of people with some cognitive handicap.

The more fundamental complication, as mentioned before, is that people can apply very different standards in their appreciation of life, and can always change them. This problem of diversity and stability may have a negative impact on the interpersonal and longitudinal comparability of cognitive happiness. It may also reduce the comparability of affective and overall happiness, due to the interaction between affective and cognitive happiness.

### *The Measurement of Overall Happiness*

The key point in measuring overall happiness is that people are not explicitly invited to report about their affective happiness, without any reflection, or to report about their cognitive happiness, after some reflection. Many questions leave room for both options, for example questions about 'happiness', without specification. A well-known question is this: *Taking all things together, how happy would you say you are?* (0–10, European Social Survey). This creates some additional freedom for adults to decide about their priorities, while young people and children probably stick to their affective happiness.

### *Problems in Measuring Overall Happiness*

The measurement of overall happiness is very similar to the measurement of cognitive happiness, and relatively easy. The additional freedom, to put priorities on either affect or cognition, might have some negative impact on the comparability of the answers. This objection is rather theoretical however, since people answer questions about cognitive and overall happiness in the same way. People answer questions about their happiness in a rather cognitive way, after some thinking or reflection. They do so if they are invited to do so, as in the ladder scale, but also without such invitation if they just get the opportunity to think first. People may also have their answers directly available, since they frequently think about their happiness.

## Reliability and Validity of the Answers

A well-known issue in happiness research is the reliability of the answers people give to questions about their happiness. It is undeniable that some people may have a tendency to be positive about their life. This can be a personal or cultural habit, but perhaps they do so deliberately, because it may work as a self-fulfilling prophecy. It can also be convenient for people, for psychological or strategic reasons, to assume they are happy, or to act as if they are happy.[11] Results of research indicate, however, that such tendencies have no serious impact on the reliability of the answers people give to happiness questions. The reliability of 'self-reported' happiness is in general very reasonable.[12]

There are also concerns about the validity of the answers people give to happiness questions. Are the answers informative for what the researchers want to know? The validity of the measurement of emotions is problematic. We would like to know how people feel, *usually*, or *in general*, but there are regular and irregular fluctuations in emotions. The answers given at specific moments, about positive and negative emotions during short periods, are not representative of affective happiness over longer periods. People's memories are not good enough to recapitulate emotions over longer periods, and there are problems with the definitions and the acceptability of positive and negative emotions.

The validity of the measurement of cognitive and overall happiness is easier because people think a lot about their lives, and there is more stability. If people are invited to think first, or if they just get the opportunity to do so, their answers will be representative of their enduring appreciation of life as a whole. We have to keep in mind, however, that children and young people will stick to their affective happiness, since their cognitive

[11] See Chap. 2: Voltaire once said: "I decided to be happy, because it is better for my health." An interesting outcome of research in this context is that florists are happier than bankers (found in Dolan, P. Happiness by Design, p. 77 (2014). Penguin Books; source: Career Happiness Index 2012). Perhaps it is more important for florists than for bankers to be happy in their contacts with clients. This might be just a matter of keeping up appearances, but might have a real impact on actual happiness eventually.

[12] Veenhoven, R. (1984). Conditions of Happiness, Chapter 3: Can happiness be measured? Dissertation. Dordrecht, Netherlands. Kluwer Academic Publishers.

and overall happiness are still 'under construction'. Perhaps they should be invited to answer different survey questions.

## Results of Empirical Research and the Typology of Happiness

Some results of empirical research deserve attention, because they invite us to have another look at the distinction between affective, cognitive and overall happiness.

(a) The correlation[13] between the self-reported levels of positive and negative emotions is obviously negative, but not very high (-0.37[14]). The reason is that mild positive and negative emotions do not exclude each other[15]; they are not opposite poles on one and the same scale. Up to a point they can go together.[16] This is different if the positive or negative emotions are very intense, as in serious depression. As noticed by Jans-Beken (2018,[17] referring to Keyes 2005[18]): "Complete mental health….consists of two related, yet distinct dimensions: psychopathology (or mental illness) and subjective well-being (or positive mental health)." The construction of an 'overall' Affect Balance Scale, as the difference between the fre-

[13]A correlation is about a relation between two factors or variables measured at an interval-level, related to an individual, a country or any other unit. If higher values in one variable go together proportionally with higher values for the other variable, then there is a positive correlation between 0 and +1; if higher values go together with lower values, the correlation is negative, between 0 and -1. A correlation (*r*) is perfect if it is +1 or -1.

[14]The correlation is -0.37 if we look at averages indices for positive and negative affect (emotions) in 156 nations in the years 2007–2019, as reported in the World Happiness Report 2020. Helliwell, J., Layard, R., & Sachs, J. (2020). World Happiness Report 2020, New York: Sustainable Development Solutions Network. (9th report, first report in 2012.) We see similar correlations at an individual level within nations, usually between -0.30 and -0.40.

[15]As observed by Pavot, W. and Diener, E. (2013). Positive and negative affect are experienced relatively independent of each other. In Chap. 10 of the Oxford Handbook of Happiness (2013), edited by David, S., Boniwell, I., and Conley Ayers, A.

[16]Diener, E. and Emmons, R. (1984)., The independence of positive and negative affect. Journal of Personality and Social Psychology, 47, 1105–1117.

[17]Jans-Beken, L. (2018). Appreciating Gratitude, New Perspectives on the Gratitude-Mental Health Connection. Open University, Heerlen, The Netherlands.

[18]Keyes, C.L., (2005). Mental illness and/or mental health? Investigating axioms of the complete state model of health. Journal of Clinical Psychology, 73(3), 539–548.

quencies of positive and negative emotions is therefore debatable. These frequencies represent information about different dynamics, possibly related to the gratification or frustration of different needs. Chronic and prominent negative emotions, in particular, can be related to the frustration of fundamental needs for safety and security in childhood. It is advisable to pay attention to the frequencies of positive and negative emotions as different indicators.

(b) It is not surprising, in this respect, that positive and negative emotions have different correlations with alternative variables. The correlation between negative emotions and cognitive happiness is rather low (-0.29), while the correlation between positive emotions and cognitive happiness is still reasonable (+0.54). The consistency between cognitive and affective happiness, at specific moments, is apparently higher for positive than for negative emotions. The correlation between emotions and other conditions is also higher for positive than for negative emotions.[19] All in all we may say that negative emotions, at least at specific moments, are more 'isolated' and less related to other current realities, than positive emotions. It would be wrong, however, to conclude that negative emotions have only a moderate impact on happiness, because the cumulative negative impact over longer periods can be strong, even if it is not reflected in any substantial correlation at specific moments. It is also possible that negative emotions have a strong negative impact on happiness, but only for a relatively small group of people.

(c) The correlation between the self-reported levels of cognitive and overall happiness is high, and much higher than the usual correlation between emotions and overall happiness.[20] This is understandable since most people give a cognitive/evaluative answer if they get

[19] The correlation with Healthy Life Expectancy, GDP, Democratic and Delivery Quality of Government, Satisfaction with Freedom and perceptions of Social Support are for Positive Affect: +0.32; +0.31; +0.38; +0.37; +0.61; +0.44. For Negative Affect the correlation is: -0.14; -0.20; -0.26; -0.27; -0.27 and -0.40.

[20] See World Happiness Report 2012, Chap. 2: "… when happiness is asked about in a life-evaluative mode, the answers have the same structures across individuals and countries as do the answers to life satisfaction questions. Indeed, these structures are so similar that taking an average of the life satisfaction and happiness answers for each respondent gives a combined evaluation of life that is explained significantly more accurately than either on its own. The same is true for life satisfaction and ladder responses in the Gallup World Poll."

questions about their overall happiness, even if they are not explicitly invited to do so. It would be incorrect however to conclude that cognition is more important for overall happiness than affect.

These results of empirical research suggest that we may apply an alternative typology of happiness, by splitting up affective happiness into positive and negative emotions, and by taking cognitive and overall happiness together as evaluative happiness. This creates a new tripartite typology: positive emotions, negative emotions, and evaluative happiness. It is also an option to take cognitive and overall happiness together as evaluative happiness, and to keep positive and negative emotions together as elements in affective happiness. Then we get a simple dichotomy with just affective and evaluative happiness.

## Focus on Evaluative Happiness

From here on we will primarily focus on evaluative happiness, either cognitive or overall, as the type of happiness to be used as a standard in our personal life and in politics. This focus will never imply, however, that cognition is supposed to be more important for happiness than affect, as has been discussed in Chap. 5. There are two arguments for focusing on evaluative happiness.

The first argument is practical and somewhat ad hoc: it is, at least for the time being, difficult to measure long-term affective happiness effectively. This measurement will probably be improved in the future, but it will take time, and even then we may expect that the measurement of evaluative happiness will always be easier.

The second argument is more fundamental. People are free to adopt and adapt their own standards to be used in the evaluation of their life as a whole. They may even put a low priority on specific emotions or their affective happiness in general. This individual freedom in evaluative happiness creates complications in research, but it makes evaluative happiness a valuable indicator because people are free to apply their own standards, based on their own values and convictions.

One of the complications associated with individual freedom, to adopt and adapt standards for the appreciation of life, is the risk of incomparability. As mentioned in the first chapter we may distinguish the more quantitative descriptive comparability from the more qualitative causal comparability. If we can explain differences in evaluative happiness with some explanatory factors, we may assume that there is causal comparability; and if there is causal comparability, we may assume that there is descriptive comparability.[21]

## Explanations of Happiness in General

Surveys with questions about happiness have produced a lot of research findings. Many findings are collected in the World Data Base of Happiness[22] and a lot of actual research is presented in the World Happiness Reports. The first Report was published in 2012. The Reports present a lot of data from different sources, like the Gallup World Poll, as indicated in the Reports. All data in this paragraph about happiness and underlying factors are retrieved from The World Happiness Report 2020.[23] The data about happiness are based on surveys in the years 2005–2019 in more than 150 nations, usually 156.

The findings have not yet produced a general theory of happiness, but have produced many explanations for specific observed differences, such as differences in average happiness between nations and in individual happiness within nations. It is important to realize that an explanation of differences in happiness is not the same as a general explanation of happiness. In an explanation of differences, we look at factors that contribute to observed differences. The implication is that even important factors are ignored, if they do not contribute to the differences. This can be the case if they always have the same impact on happiness, either positive or negative. Oxygen is important for happiness, but the percentage of oxygen in the air is not used as an explanatory factor for happiness, because the percentage of oxygen in the air is, at least for the time being, practically the same anywhere; about 21%.

[21] See footnote 22 in Chap. 1.

[22] Ibid., The WDH contains approximately 18500 correlational findings in 2000 studies (December 2019).

[23] Helliwell, John F., Richard Layard, Jeffrey Sachs, and Jan-Emmanuel De Neve, eds. 2020. World Happiness Report 2020. New York: Sustainable Development Solutions Network.Data in Excel-file WHR_DataForTable 2.1; Site https://worldhappiness.report/ed/2020/

## Explanations of Differences in Average Evaluative Happiness in Nations[24]

If we want to explain differences in average happiness in nations, we obviously have to decide what kind of data we want to use. Here we will try to explain average evaluative happiness, as measured in the Gallup World Poll with the ladder scale.[25] In a further step we must look for factors with some substantial impact on the quality of life in nations. Such factors should be related to the gratification of general human needs, and in particular to the gratification of the fundamental need for safety and security. It is not helpful to pay attention to marginal factors, like the supply of vanilla ice-cream. In this respect we may pay attention to four factors primarily related to objective realities, and four factors related to subjective realities.

Four factors, related to objective realities, have a strong correlation with average happiness.

(a) Healthy Life Expectancy (HLE).[26] Correlation r with evaluative happiness is +0.74. Healthy Life Expectancy has no direct impact on happiness, but it is a good indicator for objective safety and security, as provided by health-care, and government agencies like the police.
(b) GDP per capita[27] ($r = +0.78$). We may assume that some minimal GDP is needed for safety and security, for example to buy food and to organize health-care and safety and security.
(c) Democratic Quality of Government[28] ($r = +0.62$). This is the average score of the first two of the six Worldwide Governance

[24] See Annex for more information about variables.

[25] With a 0–10-scale, as explained in the beginning of this chapter (Measurement of cognitive (evaluative) happiness or contentment.

[26] Healthy life expectancies at birth are based on data from the World Health Organization's Global Health Observatory data repository.

[27] The statistics of GDP per capita in purchasing power parity (PPP) at constant 2011 international dollar prices are from the November 28, 2019, update of the World Development Indicators (WDI).

[28] Helliwell, J. & Huang, H. (2008). How is your government? International evidence linking good government and well-being. The British Journal of Political Science, 38, 595–619. They coined the terms Democratic and Delivery Quality for the first two and the last four Worldwide Governance Indicators (WGI) as developed by the World Bank: Kaufmann, D.; Kraay, A.; and Mastruzzi, M.; The Worldwide Governance Indicators: Methodology and Analytical Issues; in the World Bank Policy Research Working Paper No. 5430.

Indicators (WGI[29]): *Voice and Accountability* and *Political Stability and the absence of violence.*

(d) Delivery Quality of Government[30] ($r$ = +0.71). This is the average score of the last four of the six Worldwide Governance Indicators: *Government Effectiveness, Regulatory Quality, Rule of Law* and *Control of Corruption.*

The Democratic and Delivery Quality of governments are important for happiness in two ways: they are important for the creation of important conditions for happiness like security, safety and some GDP, and they are important in direct contacts between citizens and government agencies. In the next chapter there will be more discussion about the importance of government for happiness. With these four factors, related to objective realities,[31] we get a reasonable explanation of the differences in average evaluative happiness; about 66% is explained ($R$-squared is 0.66[32]). This

[29] Kaufmann., Kraay. and. Mastruzzi; (World Bank). The original data have six dimensions or indicators: *Voice and Accountability, Political Stability and Absence of Violence, Government Effectiveness, Regulatory Quality, Rule of Law*, and *Control of Corruption.* The first two indicators measure the Democratic Quality of Government. The last four indicators measure the Delivery Quality. The indicators are expressed in standard-scores (mean = zero, standard deviation = 1). The first five indicators are objective in an ontological way, because they exist outside and independent of anyone's consciousness. They are also objectively measured, independent of anyone's personal preferences or characteristics. Only the last indicator, Control of Corruption, is measuring a subjective reality because the measurement is based on perceptions of corruption. Such perceptions are obviously subjective.

[30] Ott uses the phrase 'Technical Quality' instead of 'Delivery Quality', just to indicate that this government quality is less controversial than 'Democratic Quality'. Ott, J. (2010). Good governance and happiness in nations: technical quality precedes democracy and quality beats size. Journal of Happiness Studies, 11(3), 353–368.

[31] The six dimensions or indicators are measured by experts, but with standardized checklists and procedures. The measurement of '*Control of Corruption*' is perhaps somewhat less objective than the measurement of the others, since perceptions of citizens play a role in the measurement.

[32] The percentage of all differences that can be explained, or the $R$-squared in statistical terminology, is a helpful standard to assess the effectiveness of explanations of differences in actual phenomena. If 100% of the differences can be explained, then the effectiveness is perfect. It is important to notice, however, that a low $R$-squared does not imply that we do not know anything about some phenomenon. In many situations we can still explain or predict the impact of specific factors. If the $R$-squared is low, however, we will have to be careful with general statements, because the implication is that we do not really know what is going on. A lack of information about important variables is a well-known problem (the problem of "omitted variables").

explanation is acceptable, but gets more attention in the next chapter. Statistical exercises are helpful, but are not sufficient to develop an adequate understanding of the dynamics between happiness and the factors just mentioned.

We can further improve the explanation by using two additional factors related to more subjective realities.

(e) Subjective freedom to make life choices.[33] ($r$ = +0.52)
(f) Subjective assessment of available social support, or having someone to count on in times of trouble.[34] ($r$ = +0.70)

Individual freedom and the availability of social support can be objective realities, but here they are primarily subjective, because the survey questions ask for perceptions. Such perceptions can be consistent with objective realities, but this is uncertain. If we use these two additional variables 73% instead of 66% of the differences in average, happiness in nations is explained.

It is interesting to add average frequencies of positive and negative emotions, as subjective factors measured at the same moment as the measurement of evaluative happiness.

(g) Average frequency of positive emotions.[35] The correlation r with evaluative happiness is +0.54.
(h) Average frequency of negative emotions.[36] The correlation r with evaluative happiness is -0.29.

If we add these elements of affective happiness, the variance explained goes up from 73% to 76%.

[33] This is the national average of responses to the question "Are you satisfied or dissatisfied with your freedom to choose what you do with your life?" (Gallup World Poll).

[34] This is the national average of the binary responses (either 0 or 1) to the question "If you were in trouble, do you have relatives or friends you can count on to help you whenever you need them, or not?" (Gallup World Poll).

[35] Average of three positive affect measures. "Did you experience the following feelings during a lot of the day yesterday?" (Happiness and Enjoyment). "Did you smile or laugh a lot yesterday?" (Gallup World Poll).

[36] Average of three negative affect measures. "Did you experience the following feelings during a lot of the day yesterday? (Worry, Sadness, Anger). (Gallup World Poll).

It is remarkable that differences in evaluative happiness in nations can be explained quite well with objective factors, and even better than with subjective factors. If we use the last four subjective factors together, then only 59% of the differences are explained,[37] instead of the 66% explained by the first four objective factors. Usually it is easier to explain differences in subjective factors, like happiness, with other subjective factors. Subjective factors are usually interdependent, because they are associated with genes and personality.

It would be premature, however, to conclude that objective realities are more important than subjective realities. The only correct conclusion is that differences in actual objective living conditions can explain differences in average happiness quite well, and that differences in anything else, like differences in average emotions, or in 'positivism', do not overrule the impact of differences in actual objective living conditions.[38]

We may also conclude, finally, that the explanation of average happiness in nations by objective realities is not frustrated by a lack of comparability of average happiness. The implication is that the comparability of average happiness in nations, even with different cultures, is good enough to do comparative research and statistical analysis.

[37] 56% is explained with the perceptions of freedom and available social support; 55% is explained with positive and negative emotions, and 59% by all four factors.

[38] The importance of objective living conditions for happiness in supported by research, for example by Rodriguez-Pose, A. and Maslauskaite, K. (2011). Can policy make us happier? Individual characteristics, socio-economic factors and life satisfaction in Central and Eastern Europe. Cambridge Journal of Regions, Economy and Society 2011, 1–20. Average happiness in Central- and Eastern European Nations has always been lower than in the other European nations, even after the changes in 1989. One assumption is that differences in average happiness are also an outcome of differences in innate individual characteristics. However, the authors show that there are no differences at this point between Eastern and Central European nations and the other European nations. The low levels of happiness in Central and Eastern Europe can be explained quite well with differences by institutional factors, such as the quality of government, and in particular the control of corruption as one of the dimensions of this quality.

## Explanations of Differences in Individual Evaluative Happiness Within Nations

It is difficult to formulate general statements about the explanation of differences in individual happiness within nations. There are almost 200 nations and in most nations there has been happiness research. Popular objective realities to explain individual differences are objective safety and security, individual income, education, personality characteristics, age, being married, having a partner, having a job and objective health. Popular subjective realities are subjective safety and security, subjective health, trust, religion, optimism and gratitude. Different definitions are used for all these variables.

It is impossible to summarize the results of all this research, but there is one general observation to be made. It appears to be very difficult to explain differences in individual happiness within nations. With factors related to objective realities, the percentage of explained differences is usually lower than 10%. If factors related to subjective realities are used additionally, then this percentage goes up but it usually remains below 40%. It can only get a little bit higher with subjective factors closely related to happiness, like subjective health or optimism.

The difference in the effectiveness of the explanations of average and individual happiness is remarkable. There is one trivial statistical reason: average happiness has more stability than individual happiness, since many fluctuations in individual happiness cancel each other out and are not reflected in the average. But this is not the whole story; there are more potential reasons for the low effectiveness.

(a) The differences in individual happiness in nations are relatively small, because collective conditions in nations have a substantial impact. This is in particular observable in nations with a high average happiness. In the Netherlands, with a high average, most people rate their life with an 8 on a 1–10-scale, and if it is not an 8 it is usually a 7 or a 9. So the differences are small and perhaps somewhat unstable, and therefore difficult to explain. An additional problem in this context might be that some people may have reached some maximum level of happiness; then their level of happiness will be unaffected by further improvements in their objective quality of life, and harder to explain.[39] Differences in objective quality of life, above some level, can no longer contribute to the explanation of differences in happiness. Theoretically we might encounter the same problem in the explanation of average happiness, but even in happy nations there is usually room for improvement of the average.

(b) Perhaps we have to use more and better information in the explanations, for example information about subjective realities, like emotional dispositions, genetics and mental problems. We may also have to use more and better information about the diverse impact of cognitive peculiarities and social dynamics.

(c) A more fundamental explanation might be that the interpersonal comparability of individual happiness within nations is more problematic than the comparability of average happiness in nations; see below.

## Conclusions About the Comparability of Average and Individual Happiness

### *Interpersonal Comparability*

The fact that differences in average evaluative happiness can be explained quite well is interesting because the implication is that the international comparability of happiness in nations, as a specific type of interpersonal comparability, is reasonably good. If differences in average happiness can be explained quite well with the same objective realities, then we may assume that average evaluative happiness depends on the same factors and is therefore comparable, not just in a qualitative causal way, but by implication also in a more quantitative descriptive way.[40,41]

The explanation of differences in individual evaluative happiness within nations is problematic. We may assume that there is quantitative

[39] The implication is obviously not that improvements in living conditions are irrelevant for happiness, if maximum happiness levels have been reached. Such improvements can make the high levels of happiness more robust and less vulnerable for adversity. This became clear again by the Corona-crisis in 2020: well-organized nations and rich people in poor nations were less vulnerable.

[40] See footnote 22 in Chap. 1.

[41] This conclusion is consistent with Veenhoven, R., Comparability of happiness across nations. In: School of Sociology and Social Work Journal, no 104, 2008, pp. 211–234.

descriptive comparability, because individuals can express their happiness on numerical scales, but the more qualitative causal comparability is not convincing. It is premature, however, to conclude that the ineffectiveness of the explanation is a consequence of interpersonal incomparability. There are alternative and more trivial reasons, like a lack of information about individual emotional development and mental problems. It will certainly be easier to assess the comparability if more and better information can be used in the explanation.

But perhaps we will have to accept, eventually, that incomparability is indeed one of the problems. The collective objective conditions, like the ones mentioned in the previous paragraph, contribute to individual freedom. In some nations people may use this freedom to adopt very different standards for their happiness, and may change their standards frequently. The diversity and instability in their standards might make their happiness indeterminate and immune to any rational explanation. Individual freedom has a positive impact on happiness,[42] but it is a complication for the explanation of happiness.

### *Longitudinal Comparability*

It is still difficult to assess the longitudinal comparability of happiness. The comparability of individual happiness of the same people, at different moments or in different periods, is probably acceptable if the time between such moments or periods is not too long, for example less than five years. We know that individual happiness is rather stable and this is an indication that there are no drastic changes, caused by a change in standards or otherwise.[43]

It is plausible, however, that the standards individuals apply change when they get older. Emotions probably become somewhat milder, while evaluative happiness, based on alternative standards, probably becomes more important. It is also a fact that people do change their standards

[42] Veenhoven, R.: 2008, Freedom and happiness: Comparison of 126 nations in 2006; paper presented at: Legatum Prosperity Workshop, June 21–22, London.

[43] Ehrhardt, J., Veenhoven, R., Saris, W. (2000). Stability of life-satisfaction over time. Analysis of change in ranks in a national population. Journal of Happiness Studies (1) pp. 177–205. The correlation of subsequent measurements of individual overall happiness in one year is +0.75; at least in stable nations. In the longer-term time the correlation is reduced to less than 0.5, so overall happiness is not a personal trait like personality; it is sensitive to changes in living conditions.

occasionally, after difficult periods or events in their life, like getting unemployed, an accident, a serious illness or a divorce. Here again we need more and better information to explain individual happiness and its comparability.[44]

It is also difficult to assess the longitudinal comparability of happiness over even longer periods, for example over different generations. We know that our ancestors applied different standards to evaluate their life. Future generations will certainly adopt very different standards than the current standards. We cannot assess the potential impact of such developments for the time being, because the systematic collection of data about happiness started only around 1995.

We need more information, but in the meantime it will be helpful to have another look at the effective explanation of average happiness in nations, and in particular at the important role of good governance. This will help us to find some practical possibilities for pursuing the greatest happiness for the greatest number, if we decide we want to do so.

[44] There has been a lot of qualitative research about the diversity and changeability of adult standards within nations. Just two examples. In the UK: Hyman, L. (2014). Happiness: Understandings, Narratives and Discourses. Palgrave Macmillan. In Belgium: Elchardus, M. and Smits, W. (2007) Het Grootste Geluk. LannooCampus. Panel studies can also contribute to a better understanding, but it will also be helpful to have 'big data' about the issues mentioned before, like emotional dispositions, cognitive peculiarities and mental problems.

## Annex: Information About Variables and Data Sources

*Evaluative Happiness, Measured with 'Cantril Life Ladder'*
A popular survey question to measure evaluative happiness is: 'Please imagine a ladder, with steps numbered from 0 at the bottom to 10 at the top. The top of the ladder represents the best possible life for you and the bottom of the ladder represents the worst possible life for you. On which step of the ladder would you say you personally feel you stand at this time?' This measure is also referred to as *Cantril life ladder*, or just *Life Ladder* (Gallup World Poll) *(Subjective reality)*

*Healthy Life Expectancy (HLE)*. Correlation *r* with evaluative happiness is +0.74. Healthy Life Expectancy has no direct impact on happiness but it is a good indicator for objective safety and security, as provided by health-care, some minimal GDP and government agencies like the police. Healthy life expectancies at birth are based on data from the World Health Organization's Global Health Observatory data repository.

*GDP per capita* ($r$ = +0.78). We may assume that some minimal GDP is needed for safety and security, for example to buy food and to organize healthcare and safety and security. The statistics of GDP per capita in purchasing power parity (PPP) at constant 2011 international dollar prices are from the November 28, 2019, update of the World Development Indicators (WDI).

*Democratic Quality of Government* ($r$ = +0.62). This is the average score of the first two of the six Worldwide Governance Indicators (WGI[45]):

1. *Voice and Accountability*: the extent to which a country's citizens are able to participate in selecting their government, as well as freedom of expression, freedom of association and a free media.
2. *Political Stability and Absence of Violence*: Perceptions of the likelihood that the government will be destabilized or overthrown by unconstitutional or violent means, including domestic violence and terrorism.

[45] See note 29, this Chapter.

*Delivery Quality of Government* ($r$ = +0.71). This is the average score of the last four of the six Worldwide Governance Indicators:

3. *Government effectiveness*: The quality of public services, the quality of the civil service and the degree of its independence from political pressures, the quality of policy formulations and implementation, and the credibility of the government's commitment to such policies.
4. *Regulatory Quality*: The ability of the government to formulate and implement sound policies and regulations that permit and promote private sector development.
5. *Rule of Law*: The extent to which agents have confidence in and abide by the rules of society, and in particular the quality of contract enforcement, the police and the courts, as well as the likelihood of crime and violence.
6. *Control of Corruption*: The extent to which public power is exercised for private gain, including both petty and grand forms of corruption, as well as 'capture' of the state by elites and private interests.

*Freedom to make life choices* ($r$ = +0.52). This is the national average of responses to the question 'Are you satisfied or dissatisfied with your freedom to choose what you do with your life?' (Gallup World Poll).

*Social support, or having someone to count on in times of trouble* ($r$ = +0.70). This is the national average of the binary responses (either 0 or 1) to the question 'If you were in trouble, do you have relatives or friends you can count on to help you whenever you need them, or not?' (Gallup World Poll).

*Negative affect* ($r$ = -0.29). Negative affect is defined as the average of three negative affect measures: 'Did you experience the following feelings during a lot of the day yesterday? Worry? Sadness? Anger?' (Gallup World Poll).

*Positive affect* ($r$ = +0.54). Positive affect is defined as the average of three positive affect measures: 'Did you experience the following feelings during a lot of the day yesterday? How about Happiness?' 'How about Enjoyment?' 'Did you smile or laugh a lot yesterday?' (Gallup World Poll)

## Bibliography

Cantril, H. (1965). *The pattern of human concerns.* New York: New Brunswick.

Csikzentmihalyi, M., & Hunter, J. (2003). The use of experience sampling. *Journal of Happiness Studies, 4*(2), 185–199.

Jans-Beken, L. (2018). *Appreciating gratitude, new perspectives on the gratitude-mental health connection.* Heerlen: Open University.

Kahneman, D., Kreuger, A. B., & Schkade, D. A. (2004). A survey method for characterizing daily life experience: The day reconstruction method. *Science, 306*, 1776–1780.

Keyes, C. L. (2005). Mental illness and/or mental health? Investigating axioms of the complete state model of health. *Journal of Clinical Psychology, 73*(3), 539–548.

CHAPTER 7

# Governments and Happiness

## Governments and Individual Freedom: A Sensitive Issue

The relation between individual freedom and authority on any collective level, for example in a family, a group, a company, a city, a state, a union, a political party[1] or a nation, has always been a complicated and fascinating issue. In 1651 Thomas Hobbes published his *Leviathan*, three years after the Peace of Westphalia and Munster, putting an end to two bloody wars with a lot of misery: the Thirty Years' War between Catholic and Protestant powers; and the Eighty Years' War between the Protestant Dutch Republic and Catholic Spain. *Leviathan* was based on the assumption that peace and stability deserve the highest priority. Hobbes believed that sovereigns, such as kings, should have absolute power, with a firm monopoly on violence, to create safety and stability. Citizens have the right of opposition, but only if a sovereign fails to deliver this.

In 1690 John Locke published *Two Treatises of Government* with arguments for establishing more rights for citizens: they should be entitled to safety, but also to liberty and property as their means for survival.

[1] An old but still interesting theory in this context is that complex democratic organizations, like trade unions and political parties, will always develop into oligarchies; with problematic consequences for the relation between individual members and leaders. This is the "Iron Law of the Oligarchy" by Michels, R. 1911. A Sociological Study of the Oligarchical Tendencies of Modern Democracy. New York: The Free Press.


J. Ott, *Beyond Economics*,
https://doi.org/10.1007/978-3-030-56600-5_7

Governments must create safety and stability, but should also protect such 'survival rights'.

*De l'Esprit des Lois* (1748) by Charles Montesquieu was based on his philosophy that *government should be set up so that no man needs to be afraid of another* and that such a government needs a balanced and clearly defined separation of three main powers: the legislative, executive and judicial power.

Jean-Jacques Rousseau argued in his *Du contrat social ou principes du droit politique* (1762), that a government can do anything if it is consistent with the 'general will' of the citizens. He did not define this 'general will', but the message is that citizens have to accept whatever a government wants, as long as this 'general will' is respected. This philosophy was one of the leading principles in the French Revolution, starting in 1789, with the guillotine as a practical instrument. It was important for the French Constitution of 1792 and has been a convenient philosophy in totalitarian ideologies.

We must immediately add that this philosophy of Rousseau is based on the assumption of perfect democracy. His philosophy is against the absolute power of any sovereign. It is about a fictional contract between citizens, and not about a fictional contract between a sovereign and his people, as in the philosophies of Hobbes and Locke.

Hobbes, Locke and Rousseau put a high priority on the effectiveness of the power of some central authority, like a king, a state or a government. Montesquieu was more careful at this point with his plea for a separation of powers. His work influenced the American founders, and in particular James Madison. This is understandable because many people who went to the US in the seventeenth and eighteenth century wanted to get away from repression by autocratic European regimes. The quest for freedom in the US is still visible in many monuments and museums in Washington and Philadelphia, like the Washington museum, the Independence Hall with the nearby National Constitution Center and the Liberty Bell.

Oppression by totalitarian regimes, as reflected in the horrors of the Second World War and in communism, contributed in many nations to a higher priority for individual human rights and support for decolonization. In 1948 the General Assembly of the United Nations proclaimed the General Declaration of Human Rights, with 30 articles; establishing many rights of citizens in relation to their government, but also many general rights that should be protected by their governments. Occasionally a distinction is made between individual negative and positive rights. Negative rights imply that individuals should have their private space, not to be trespassed by their government or any other organization. Positive rights imply that individuals are entitled to active support by their government to get some important services; for example, they should be entitled to medical care, education and employment.

Perhaps we may say that individual freedom has become more important since the American independence. In economics this development has eventually culminated in the ideology of neo-liberalism. There are different variants and interpretations, but the common denominator is that governments should be small and modest. In the more radical variants there should be no government at all, to create maximum freedom.

Friedrich Hayek is one of the pioneers of this ideology. In *The Road to Serfdom*, published in 1944,[2] he argues that governments have a strong tendency to become bigger and more powerful, with eventually disastrous effects for individual freedom. The Chicago School of Economics, with representatives like Milton Friedman,[3] formalised this economic theory and Margaret Thatcher and Ronald Reagan put it into practice. Nowadays it has become a leading theory in most nations.

It is obviously wise to be critical about governments. Relations between citizens and government agencies are not based on equality and consensus, but on hierarchy. It is therefore essential that the quality of governments is very high, and that citizens can protect themselves against questionable decisions. People want to be treated carefully, respectfully and without discrimination. It is also important that governments are not overambitious, because this may lead to indifference and apathy among citizens.

In the next paragraphs we can show that good governments make a difference and how it works. There is no need for big governments, but the quality must be high.

[2] Hayek, F. The Road to Serfdom (1944). Routledge Press, University of Chicago Press.
[3] Friedman, M. Capitalism and Freedom (1962). University of Chicago Press.

## The Importance of Government Quality for Happiness in Nations

People tend to believe that the impact of government on happiness is low. Headey and Wearing (1992)[4] found that people estimate that governments contribute less to happiness than any other potential source. Such beliefs are understandable, since people are primarily interested in differences in happiness in their own environment. Such differences are not related to common conditions as such, but to individual differences or to the interaction between common conditions and individual characteristics. Governments may have some impact on individual differences, but they are primarily responsible for the man-made common living conditions.

The differences in average (evaluative) happiness in nations are very substantial, usually between 2 and 8 on a 0–10-scale. In 2019 there is a minimum of 2.37 for Afghanistan and a maximum of 7.78 for Finland.[5] The differences in individual happiness within nations are usually less substantial, in particular in rich nations with a relatively high average. Many people in rich and developed nations rate their life with a 7.8 or 9, and there is only a relatively small minority of unhappy people.

The combination of a high average with a high level of equality is not surprising for a trivial statistical reason: many people have to be happy to get a high average, and the differences in happiness will have to be small. It is interesting, however, at least for pessimists and sceptics, that there are indeed nations with this combination of a high average and equality of individual happiness. There is no empirical justification for pessimism or scepticism in this respect.

Perhaps people's views on governments would be more accurate, if they were acquainted with the differences in average happiness and with the high correlation between average happiness and government quality, mentioned in the previous chapter. The World Bank evaluates each year six dimensions of the quality of governments in nations. The results are known as the Worldwide Government Indicators (WGI[6]) and some results

[4] Headey, B. & Wearing, A., (1992). Understanding Happiness: A theory of subjective well-being. Longman Cheshire Pty Limited. Melbourne, Australia.

[5] Helliwell, J., Layard, R., & Sachs, J. World Happiness Report 2020, New York: Sustainable Development Solutions Network. (Site: https://worldhappiness.report/ed/2020/, Data in Excel-file WHR_DataForTable2.1)

[6] Kaufmann, D.; Kraay, A.; and Mastruzzi, M.; The Worldwide Governance Indicators: Methodology and Analytical Issues; in the World Bank Policy Research Working Paper No. 5430.

are also reported in the World Happiness Reports. The six dimensions or indicators are: *Voice and Accountability*, *Political Stability and the Absence of Violence*, *Government Effectiveness*, *Regulatory Quality*, *Rule of Law*, and *Control of Corruption* (see previous chapter and Annex for more information). In the World Happiness Reports the six indicators are split up into two groups.

Delivery Quality[7] is particularly important. This quality is the average score for the last four indicators. A better Delivery Quality contributes in a rather linear way to average happiness in nations. The only condition is that this Delivery Quality must have some minimal level first, before the correlation starts. This is understandable: average happiness is not going up or down easily, and some minimum government influence is needed before anything can be accomplished.

The Democratic Quality of governments is also important for happiness. This quality is the average score for the first two indicators. The relation with average happiness is more complicated: the introduction of democracy apparently creates problems first; at low levels we see a negative or low relation, before the relation becomes positive and substantial at higher levels.

The correlation between average evaluative happiness and Delivery and Democratic Quality in the years 2007–2019 is very stable at +0.71 and +0.62, respectively.[8] Both government qualities contribute eventually to more equality in happiness. We know that rising quality goes together with social-economic improvements. If the improvements start at a low level, there will be more inequality first, because some people will benefit more than others even if government is not corrupt. If governments continue to improve, and pay more attention to people who are left behind, average happiness can continue to go up, but now with a reduction of inequality. Many nations have achieved a high average happiness with a low level of inequality.

The correlation between government quality and happiness was already established in the previous chapter; but the question is: what is the explanation, and is it a matter of causality?

[7] Helliwell, J. & Huang, H. (2008). How is your government? International evidence linking good government and well-being. The British Journal of Political Science, 38, 595–619. They coined the terminology Democratic and Delivery Quality of government.

[8] World Happiness Report 2020.

## How Do Good Governments Contribute to Happiness?

The qualities of governments are important for happiness in two different ways; they can produce direct and indirect effects.

### *Direct Effects*

Governments can have direct effects on happiness in contacts between government agencies and citizens. It is very important that in such contacts citizens are treated carefully, respectfully and without discrimination. Government agencies must apply general principles of good governance.[9] This is what Frey and Stutzer (2005) refer to as *procedural utility*.[10] This procedural utility depends heavily on the Democratic Quality of governments, but also on Rule of Law and Control of Corruption as dimensions of Delivery Quality. At this point we may say that there is a direct causal relation between government qualities and happiness.

### *Indirect Effects*

Governments can have indirect effects on happiness by creating favourable conditions for the pursuit of happiness, for example safety and security, healthcare, education, gender equality, some purchasing power, employment and safe money. In this way governments can create individual freedom and autonomy, by maintaining stable and predictable conditions that enable people to make their own life plans.

Governments can also organize some supervision of the functioning of markets, through anti-trust policies and by paying attention to the safety, minimal quality and availability of important products, like water, medicine and services such as professional advice for people with serious physical or mental problems. If needed, governments can organize some public

[9] Well-known examples are: carefulness and accuracy of decisions, respecting all interests, accounting for decisions, fair-play and equality (equal situations are treated equally), respect for reasonable expectations, no 'detournement de pouvoir' (powers have to be used in accordance with their legal background), proportionality (no disproportional negative consequences for citizens, relative to public interests). Most nations have adopted such principles, either in a specific code or in jurisprudence.

[10] Frey, B. S., & Stutzer, A. (2005). Beyond outcomes: Measuring procedural utility. Oxford, UK: Economic Papers.

services like public transport and waste treatment. This is what Frey and Stutzer (2005) refer to as *output utility*. This output utility depends heavily on Government effectiveness and Regulatory Quality, as dimensions of Delivery Quality. Such qualities are always important, but particularly in case of emergencies like a pandemic or epidemic.

We may say that many factors which contribute to happiness, or facilitate the pursuit of happiness, are up to a point intermediate factors between happiness and the qualities of government. In real life, however, there are always exceptional situations. Just as an example: some nations became very rich by exploiting natural resources like oil. In such situations wealth and a high GDP are not just intermediates between government qualities and happiness. In such situations wealth may have a direct impact on happiness independent of the government, for example, by providing for better education and medical care, possibly abroad. Wealth may even have a positive impact on the quality of the government, if this wealth is used to hire experts and consultants. As a generalization we may say, however, that the qualities of governments are usually starting points for the development of favourable conditions for happiness.[11] Such qualities have a direct impact on happiness in relations with citizens, and an indirect impact through intermediate factors.

## Quality Beats Size!

It is important to notice that the quality of governments is more important for happiness than the size, for example in terms of expenditure or numbers of civil servants. The impact of the quality of governments on happiness is independent of their size, while the impact of size on happiness depends for a great deal on the quality (Ott 2010).[12] Good governments can achieve a lot with consultation and intelligent legislation. As an example: governments can make legislation to make sure that everybody gets decent insurance for medical treatment, and leave it to private organizations to work this out. More government expenditure, or more civil

[11] Kaufmann, D. (2005). Back to basics, 10 myths about governance and corruption. Finance and Development, 42 (3). (Myth 4). He made the following observation about causality in the relation between governance and wealth: "In fact, the evidence points to the causality being in the direction of better governance leading to higher economic growth."

[12] Ott, J. (2010). Good governance and happiness in nations: technical quality precedes democracy and quality beats size. Journal of Happiness Studies, 11(3), 353–368.

servants, is usually not needed. Quality, and some other characteristics of political systems, is probably more important for happiness than the size of governments.[13]

## Governments and Individual Freedom, Sensitive but Manageable

Individual freedom is one of the factors that may be seen as an intermediate factor between government and happiness, but it is a special one.

Veenhoven[14] defines freedom as the actual individual possibility to choose, and this possibility depends on two dimensions: the opportunity to choose and the individual capability to choose.[15] Opportunity is a characteristic of the social environment and can be interpreted as the absence of inhibitions and the availability of options. In this context options and inhibitions are supposed to be 'man-made'. Capability—or capacity—is a characteristic of individuals: they must at least have some understanding of the situation and some courage to take decisions and to use their opportunities.[16]

This conceptual model is logical, but people usually just think and talk about the opportunity to choose, without much attention to the importance of relevant capacities.[17] Fred McMahon of the Fraser Institute

[13] It is interesting that some characteristics of political systems have a positive impact on happiness: average happiness is higher in nations with a parliamentary (rather than presidential) executive, a proportional representation electoral system (as opposed to single member districts), and a unitary (rather than federal) governmental structure. Such characteristics probably have a moderating impact on polarization and a positive impact on political deliberations and discussions. See: Altman, D.; Flavin, P.; Radcliff, B.F. (2016). Democratic Institutions and Subjective Well-Being. Political Studies, 2016, 1–20.

[14] Veenhoven, R. (2008). Freedom and happiness: Comparison of 126 nations in 2006. Paper presented at Legatum prosperity workshop, June 21–22, London.

[15] Concept developed by Sen. Sen, A. (1999). Development as freedom. Oxford: Oxford University Press.

[16] Christan Bay refers to this capability with his concept of Psychological Freedom. Bay, C. (1958). The structure of freedom. Stanford, CA: Stanford University Press.

[17] Is Freedom Just About the Absence of Inhibitions, or Also About the Availability of Options? Discussion Between Fred McMahon of the Fraser Institute and Jan Ott of the Erasmus University Rotterdam. Social Indicators Research, (2019) 142:305–309.

explains the views of some famous authors at this point.[18] Berlin[19] explicitly leaves capacity out of his conceptualization of freedom, with his observation that it would be eccentric to say that people are less free if they are unable to jump more than ten feet in the air, or cannot read because they are blind, or cannot understand the darker pages of Hegel. Such inhibitions are not man-made and it would be very contentious to describe such inhibitions as a lack of freedom.

Rawls[20] also explicitly adopts this approach and stipulates that the value of freedom depends on individual capacities, but that this dependence has no impact on the level of freedom as such. This approach to leave capacities out of the definition of freedom, and to concentrate on the opportunity to choose, is understandable and acceptable.

It is less understandable, and more problematic, to define this opportunity to choose exclusively in a negative way, as just the absence of inhibitions. This opportunity, as a characteristic of the environment, depends also on the availability of options. Options and inhibitions go together; they are always intertwined. Legislation creates combinations of inhibitions and options, and if there is a list of inhibitions people may assume that activities not mentioned on the list are options. Buying a car creates options to travel, even if there are certain inhibitions to be observed in driving it. The key question is: what is the balance between options and inhibitions? We can never assess individual freedom if we ignore either options or inhibitions.[21]

Most data about freedom, however, are primarily about negative freedom, as the opportunity to choose, and only as determined by the absence of inhibitions. The availability of options and capabilities is usually ignored. This is very clear in the measurement by Freedom House[22] of Personal Autonomy and Global Freedom, as the sum-score of Political Rights and

[18] McMahon, F. (2012). Human freedom from Pericles to measurement. The Independent Review: A Journal of Political Economy, 19(1), 65–84.

[19] Berlin, I. (1958). Two concepts of liberty. In Berlin (author) and Hardy (Ed.) (2002). Liberty: Incorporating four essays on liberty. Oxford: Oxford University Press.

[20] Rawls, J. (1971). A theory of justice. Cambridge: Harvard University Press.

[21] See Ott, J. and McMahon, F., (2018). Is freedom just about the absence of inhibitions, or also about the availability of options? Published on line in Social Indicators Research, https://doi.org/10.1007/s11205-018-1897-0.

[22] https://freedomhouse.org/

Civil Liberties, and in the measurement of Economic Freedom by the Fraser Institute[23] and the Heritage Foundation.[24]

There is nevertheless a substantial correlation between this negative freedom and happiness, and between negative freedom and quality of government.[25] The correlation of Global Freedom with happiness and Delivery Quality is resp. +0.53 and +0.72. The correlation of Personal Autonomy with happiness and the Delivery Quality is resp. +0.60 and +0.80.[26] The correlation between economic freedom and happiness and Delivery Quality is +0.46 and +0.78 for the Fraser Institute and +0.54 and +0.86 for the Heritage Foundation. There is also substantial correlation between average subjective freedom, defined as satisfaction with the freedom to choose what you do with your life, and average happiness (+0.52), and between this subjective freedom and Delivery Quality of government in nations (+0.48).[27]

[23] http://www.freetheworld.com.

[24] http://www.heritage.org/index.

[25] It is interesting, by the way, that there is always correlation between different types of freedom in one nation; usually they go together. This is not 'self-evident', because types of freedom can be more important for specific groups. More negative freedom, or absence of inhibitions, will be more important for people with money and power (no interference please!); more positive freedom, or availability of options, will be more important for poor people (more public goods and services please!); more economic freedom will be more important for employers, the self-employed and investors (just rule of law, no regulations please!); more private freedom and personal autonomy will be more important for cultural, religious and sexual minorities (more equality and tolerance please!). Such differences in the appreciation of freedom are apparently not inconsistent with a high mutual correlation. One reason is that there is usually some overlap in (sub-) indicators in the measurement of different freedoms. There is also a more theoretical explanation: it is eventually always about the individual freedom to make decisions, and we may expect that individuals will claim similar levels of freedom, whatever the decisions at stake. A certain level of individual freedom or autonomy can easily become a general cultural standard.

[26] Data for 2010–2012 for 127 nations; in: Ott, J. Measuring Economic Freedom: Better Without Size of Government. Soc Indic Res 135, 479–498 (2018). https://doi.org/10.1007/s11205-016-1508-x. Global freedom is the sum-score for Political Rights and Civil Liberties. Political Rights and Civil Liberties can be affected by both state and non-state actors, including insurgents and other armed groups. Examples Political Rights: right to vote, compete for public office and elect representatives. Examples Civil Liberties: freedom of expression and belief, associational and organizational rights. Examples of Personal Autonomy: freedom of travel or choice of residence, employment, or institution of higher education, right to own property and establish private business, social freedoms, including gender equality, choice of marriage partners and size of family.

[27] Data found in World Happiness Report 2020. See previous chapter for details.

The correlation between freedom and happiness is no surprise; with more individual freedom we may expect more consistency between preferences and actual lifestyles. The correlation between freedom and quality of government is no surprise either, because freedom obviously depends on government qualities like Voice and Accountability and Rule of Law. It is a surprise, however, that the correlation is already quite substantial, while freedom is measured in a narrow way, primarily as negative freedom by the absence of inhibitions.

At this point it is important to realize that the quality of government, and in particular Regulatory Quality and Government Effectiveness, is important for the level of GDP (purchasing power per capita), Life-expectancy at birth (via safety and the organization of health-care) and education, for example as expressed in average years of education per capita. Information about such factors is collected in the Human Development Index[28] of the UN (United Nations Development Programme, UNDP). These factors contribute to the development of capabilities in nations, but also to the availability of options in general. The shortcomings of a narrow measurement of freedom, as merely negative freedom due to the absence of inhibitions, can be compensated for by information about such factors.

We repeat that there is a positive relation between freedom and happiness, and between freedom and government quality, even if freedom is just defined in a narrow way as the opportunity to choose, with an emphasis on the absence of inhibitions.[29] The relation between freedom and happiness and government quality is even stronger in view of the fact that governments are also important for capabilities and the availability of options in general.

[28] http://hdr.undp.org/en/content/human-development-index-hdi

[29] The measurement of economic freedom is indeed better if it is defined in a comprehensive way, and not just in a negative way. The Fraser Institute and the Heritage Foundation assume that government activities have a negative impact on freedom because they contribute to more regulation and taxation, with more inhibitions. The level of government activities is expressed in factors like government consumption, transfers and subsidies, tax-rates (Fraser) and Government spending and fiscal freedom (Heritage). Such factors are used as negative indicators for freedom, but this is premature. If we leave out such factors, we get a better measurement with a higher internal consistency (higher Cronbach Alpha) and a higher correlation with other types of freedom and happiness. This result supports the conclusion in the previous paragraph that the Size of Government as such is not important for happiness; the impact depends on the quality of the government. See Ott, J. Measuring Economic Freedom: Better Without Size of Government. *Social Indicators Research* 135, 479–498 (2018). https://doi.org/10.1007/s11205-016-1508-x.

The fact that higher government quality goes together with more freedom and happiness is an indication that the relation between government and individual freedom can be managed, by taking good care of the quality of government.

## Conclusions

In terms of happiness there is no justification for an anti-government attitude. Good governments have a substantial positive impact on average happiness in nations. It is understandable, nevertheless, that people are critical about governments. Relations with government agencies are based on hierarchy and not on consensus and equality. Governments must respect the separation and independence of the three main powers in society: the legislative, executive and judicial power. They must also respect and apply the general principles of good governance in their contacts with citizens and non-government organizations.

Governments can also create apathy and dependency if they are overambitious. Regular contacts between government representatives and interest-groups can help to create clarity and to avoid misunderstandings about responsibilities. However, governments must always be able to act if things go wrong.

There is one caveat. It is practical that citizens and private organisations, as a rule, take care of their own interests. This assumption is still the backbone of neo-liberalism. It is also generally accepted that national governments primarily take care for their own national interests and the interests of their citizens. Government representatives get paid quite well to do so. As a consequence governments of fully developed nations are very effective in protecting and promoting such interests, for example, in international trade relations. Governments of less developed nations are substantially less effective.

Perhaps we should be more critical at this point. Adam Smith was sceptical about happiness as a general goal, for the practical reason that 'man' can only be responsible for the care of his own happiness, of that of his family, his friends and his county. We may wonder, however, whether this excuse implies that governments are entitled to take care of their own national interests only, without additional moral considerations.[30] The role

[30] See footnote in the Introduction: Smith, A. (First version in 1759; last version in 1790) Theory of Moral Sentiments. Dover Publications, Inc. Mineola, New York. See page 238:

of government has become more important again, in spite of neo-liberalism, as a result of the Corona pandemic. Governments are compelled to moderate the negative impact with substantial financial interventions. According to some economists governments should seize the opportunity to stimulate and steer the economy, for example, with investments to reduce climate change. A reduction of poverty and unhappiness in poor nations can be added as an additional purpose.[31]

## Bibliography

Frey, B. S., & Stutzer, A. (2005). *Beyond outcomes: Measuring procedural utility.* Oxford: Economic Papers.

Headey, B., & Wearing, A. (1992). *Understanding happiness: A theory of subjective well-being.* Melbourne: Longman Cheshire Pty Limited.

Ott, J. (2010). Good governance and happiness in nations: Technical quality precedes democracy and quality beats size. *Journal of Happiness Studies, 11*(3), 353–368.

"The administration of the great system of the universe, however, the care of universal happiness of all rational and sensible beings, is the business of God, and not of man. To man is allotted a much humbler department, but one much more suitable to the weakness of his powers, and to the narrowness of his comprehension- the care of his own happiness, of that of his family, his friends, his country…".

[31] For example Mazzucato, M. and Skidelsky, R. (2020). Toward a new fiscal constitution. Project Syndicate; https://www.project-syndicate.org/

CHAPTER 8

# Happiness as a Descriptive Standard or as a Standard to be Pursued

## The Reduction of Confusion About Happiness: A Summary

The introductory chapter mentioned some old and new ambiguities concerning the concept of happiness and the nature of happiness as an actual phenomenon. Such ambiguities create confusion and have a negative impact on the effectiveness of deliberations and discussions. In view of the widely accepted definition of happiness, and in view of the results of value-free research, we may now propose some options to reduce the confusion. Together these options may contribute to a better general understanding of happiness.

## Reduction of Confusion by the Current Definition

The current definition describes happiness as the appreciation by individuals of their own life as a whole. Emotions and emotional states, as elements of short- and long-term affective happiness, play a crucial role in this appreciation, particularly if individuals are still young. This affective happiness, or hedonic level of affect, will always be important as a standard in the appreciation of life, but as people grow older they will adopt new standards, about issues like appearance, social behaviour, religious and political convictions, sustainability, developing their talents and making money. The relative importance of the hedonic level of affect will


J. Ott, *Beyond Economics*,
https://doi.org/10.1007/978-3-030-56600-5_8

diminish, but a minimal hedonic level of affect or emotional well-being is always needed as a condition for development and functioning.

The new definition resolves some ambiguities. Happiness is not about the appreciation of some specific issues or domains of life, it is not some short-term emotion or some perfect state, and it is not the same as the economic notion of utility. Happiness is subjective, has a maximum and is primarily based on experiences. Utility is also subjective, but strongly related to objective characteristics of commodities and services. Utility is unlimited because it is expressed in expenditures that may go up without any limits. Many expenditures are based on expectations, or expected utility.

With the current definition it is also clear that happiness is not by definition morally acceptable or unacceptable. Certain theories, and in particular Aristotelian theories, hold that happiness and well-being are by definition virtuous or dependent on virtue.[1] This is not a feature of the current definition, which does not rule out the possibility that people may achieve happiness, individually or collectively, through an immoral way of life. People may adopt peculiar standards and may pursue happiness in debatable ways. It is also impracticable to incorporate morality in the definition, because it would make it virtually impossible to assess or measure such happiness.[2]

This is not an excuse to ignore morality dilemmas related to happiness. We can be more specific. Happiness can be immoral in two ways: it can be immoral if it is the only standard to be applied, and it can be immoral by inconsistency with some alternative standard. The second type of potential immorality will be discussed later, but the first type deserves some attention right here.

Happiness can be based on behaviour with negative consequences for the happiness of other people. An individual in a group can gain happiness by making unpleasant jokes about other individuals in the group; individuals in a group can gain happiness by making unpleasant jokes about one of the members (bullying); hooligans can gain happiness by being very unpleasant to other hooligans, the public, the police and so on. We

[1] For example: Kraut, R. (2007). What is Good and Why, Cambridge, MA. and London: Harvard University Press, p. 196: "Justice in relation to the whole of one's social world is one component of a flourishing life; if someone is entirely unjust—unjust to everyone—that by itself detracts from his well-being."

[2] See Ott, J. (2013). Science and morality: Mind the gap, use happiness as a safe bridge! Journal of Happiness Studies, Vol. 14(1), pp. 345–351.

may even add that, arguably, a high average happiness in a nation can be based on an immoral lifestyle or on immoral policies, with a disproportionate use of natural resources, disproportionate pollution and unfair trade relations with poor nations.

It is a substantial comfort, however, that happier people are in general better citizens, in terms of empathy and social and moral behaviour.[3] This is understandable: if people are happy, they probably have no serious problems and more time and energy for social relations and new challenges. We may conclude that the ambiguity about the morality of happiness is resolved with the current definition. Happiness is not by definition morally acceptable, or altruistic or egocentric. Happiness in practice is usually based on morally acceptable behaviour, but there are exceptions and we have to be critical.

## Using the Results of Value-Free Research to Reduce Confusion

There has been a lot of research related to happiness as defined. The results have contributed to a better understanding and an additional reduction of ambiguities, for example, about the meaning of happiness, internal consistency and comparability.

1. *Meaning*

   The meaning of the word 'happiness' is sometimes unclear, if it is used without any specification. It is wise, in view of research results, to use the word 'happiness' first of all for evaluative happiness. People have a natural tendency to think first before they answer questions about their happiness. Usually they even have their answers directly available, because they frequently think about their life as a whole. Their appreciation of life is based on some cognitive activity and on the application of standards. It is therefore realistic to assume that self-reported happiness is evaluative, unless otherwise specified. The situation is somewhat different for children, because their happiness is only or primarily based on affect.

2 *Consistency*

   Happiness is evaluative and the implication is that happiness is more than just how you feel. People attribute different weights and

[3] Guven, C. (2011). Are happier people better citizens? Kyklos, 64 (2), 178–192.

meanings to their feelings or emotions. It would be wrong, and perhaps even paternalistic, to ignore this attribution.[4] But emotions are nevertheless crucial for evaluative happiness. High frequencies of positive emotions, and low frequencies of intense negative emotions, in childhood or later, are a condition for emotional and cognitive development. Emotions are somehow integrated into the overall appreciation of life, and this integration contributes to consistency between affective and cognitive happiness. This consistency is the justification for the notions of 'overall' and 'evaluative' happiness.

3. *Two typologies or one dichotomy*

   The first typology we introduced and used is: overall happiness, with affective and cognitive happiness as components. One result of research is that cognitive as well as overall happiness are based on some cognitive appraisal. We may take them together as evaluative happiness. Another result of research is that positive and negative emotions have their own dynamics. It is therefore acceptable to split affective happiness up into positive and negative emotions. In this way we get an alternative typology:

   (a) Evaluative happiness, or just happiness, based on some cognitive appraisal of one's own life as a whole.
   (b) Positive emotions, rather common and related to happiness; facilitate cognitive and emotional development.
   (c) Negative emotions, more exceptional and isolated; possibly with a serious negative impact on current or future happiness. Serious problems in physical or mental health can be a reason.

   We may also apply a simple dichotomy of affective and evaluative happiness, if we do not split affective happiness into positive and negative emotions.

[4]This is an interesting fundamental point in discussions about well-being: the maximization of aggregated individual benefits can be disputable since people may put different priorities on conditions and positive or negative emotions. This is a potential problem if the valuation of emotions by the people themselves is disregarded. There is no such problem if evaluative happiness is used as a standard, because people decide themselves about the standards they want to apply in their evaluation of their life, and in their evaluation of specific conditions and emotions.

4. *Interpersonal comparability*

   The interpersonal comparability of happiness, of different people at the same moments or during the same periods of time, is another complication. In view of research results we may conclude that average happiness is reasonably comparable between different nations, but comparing individual happiness within nations is more difficult.
5. *Longitudinal comparability*

   The longitudinal comparability of happiness, of the same people at different moments or in different periods, is also complicated. The happiness of a single person is in general reasonably comparable for periods no longer than five years, but less predictable within longer periods. People do change their standards if they get older. It is impossible to assess the comparability of average happiness of different generations, because there is not enough information.

## Value-Free Arguments to Accept or Reject Happiness as a Standard

We can make a list of arguments in favour of happiness as a standard (pros), and a list of arguments for being cautious (cons). These arguments are value-free, but in one of the next paragraphs we can discuss some normative aspects of happiness as a standard. The arguments are relevant to happiness as a descriptive standard, but a fortiori also to happiness as a standard to be pursued. All arguments are relevant to happiness in general, but the argument that it is easy to collect information about happiness only applies to evaluative happiness. The collection of information about affective happiness, and about long-term affective happiness in particular, is complicated.

### *List of Pros*

There are arguments in favour of happiness as a standard.

(a) *It is easy and cheap to collect information about evaluative happiness*

   It is easy and relatively cheap to collect information about evaluative happiness with a few survey questions, like the ladder scale. Information about evaluative happiness can help detect personal or social-economic problems, and can be a good basis for further research and policy development. More specifically, it can produce information about the relative importance of problems people have to deal with. Policy-makers and politicians may assume that people have specific problems and priorities, but the subjective experience of the people concerned can be different.

(b) *Popularity*

Happiness, as a specific type of subjective well-being, is highly appreciated by most people. There are other popular goals and standards, but happiness is always on top of the list. It is difficult to ignore it.

(c) *Dependence on objective standards must be limited*

Objective standards, measuring objective well-being, are developed by experts. Such standards are somewhat arbitrary and not value-free. Reliance on the usual economic standards, like GDP, income, profits, paid employment and consumption, has become contentious in high-productivity nations. It is wise to apply subjective indicators, measuring subjective well-being, to get a more comprehensive and accurate picture. Happiness as subjective well-being, or as a subjective standard for well-being, can fulfil this function. A very practical point in this context is that happiness is the most appropriate subjective standard, and perhaps even the only appropriate subjective standard, to be used worldwide. People all over the world think regularly about their happiness, as their appreciation of life. There are no alternative topics receiving a similar amount of attention. People also think a lot about their safety, job, health, income, partner and children. But it depends very much on their situation how much they think about such topics. Some people have no job, partner or children. The attention to happiness as subjective well-being, however, is universal and independent of personal situations. If we want a subjective standard to be generally applicable, then happiness is the most appropriate candidate.

(d) *Happiness as a universal standard facilitates interdisciplinary research*

Social sciences have explicit or implicit theories about well-being. Such theories, for example medical, psychological or economic theories, are typically based on specific standards as elements in more comprehensive theories, for example, related to blood quality, neuroticism and welfare. Such theories are often about objective well-being, that is well-being as assessed by observers and not as experienced by the people themselves, applying their own standards. It would be helpful if social sciences paid more attention to happiness as subjective well-being. In this way subjective well-being could function as a common denominator.

(e) *Happiness as a universal standard compensates for limits in empathy*
As observed by Adam Smith: human empathy is limited. Happiness as a universal standard may help us to compensate for this shortcoming.

### *List of Cons*

There are also arguments for caution about happiness as a standard.

(a) *Information about happiness is usually incomplete*
It is true that it is easy to collect and analyse information about evaluative happiness, but in the current surveys some issues have been neglected, particularly issues related to long-term affective happiness, such as emotional dispositions, development, mental problems and inconsistencies in happiness. People are able to give general answers if questions about their happiness are asked, but there can be inconsistencies, for example, between positive and negative emotions, between emotions and cognitive evaluation, and between different standards to be applied in the appreciation of life as a whole. People may ignore such inconsistencies, if they report about their happiness, but it would be helpful to have more information about such issues for a correct interpretation of the answers.

(b) *Whose happiness as a standard?*
The practical utility of happiness as a standard is limited. It is not a panacea. If happiness is accepted as a standard, people still have to decide about priorities. Whose happiness deserves priority? Their own happiness? The happiness of people in their personal environment, in their household or family, in their own national society, or in the world as a whole? And do they put priority on current or future happiness, or on the happiness of future generations? We must acknowledge that even with happiness as a standard, there are still many decisions to be made about priorities. We have the

option, however, to use happiness as a standard or indicator only in a descriptive way; detecting unhappiness and problems, but without conclusions about priorities.

(c) *Relation between happiness and actual conditions can be illogical*

People adapt their standards. They get more critical if life is easy and less critical if life is hard. They may also decide that they are happy, or to act as if they are happy, for strategic or psychological reasons. Happiness also has a maximum (see point e below). The relation between actual conditions and happiness is therefore not self-evident. We may expect that the scores on happiness scales are somewhat condensed. The lower scores can be somewhat high relative to actual conditions if people in bad conditions become less critical. The high scores can be relatively low if people become more critical and if the high scores are close to their maximum. The fact that people adapt their standards for happiness may never be an excuse, as argued by Sen[5] and Nussbaum,[6] to disregard or neglect problems in actual objective living conditions.

(d) *Unhappiness can be natural, functional and inevitable*

Some unhappiness can be a natural and inevitable consequence of some personal or social-economic development. Growing up and getting older may have unpleasant consequences from time to time, and social-economic developments may have positive effects for some people, but negative effects for others. Such consequences can be inevitable in some stages of development. It could still be helpful to detect such unhappiness, but the practical importance might be limited.

(e) *Happiness is a dynamic phenomenon, and it has a maximum*

Individual and average happiness have a maximum. The implication is that improvements in actual conditions are no longer reflected in more individual or average happiness, if this maximum has been reached.[7] The implication is not, however, that such

[5] Sen, A. (1999). Capabilities and Commodities. Oxford, UK. Oxford University Press.

[6] Nussbaum, A. (2000). Women and Development. Cambridge, UK. Cambridge University Press.

[7] Easterlin found that economic growth has no substantial impact anymore on happiness in rich nations. If such nations have (almost) reached their 'natural' maximum, then this can be one of the explanations. In: Easterlin, R. (1974). Does economic growth improve the human lot? Some empirical evidence. In David, P.A. & Reder, W. (Eds.) Nations and households in economic growth: Essays in honour of Moses Abramowitz. New York, NY, Academic Press.

improvements are irrelevant for happiness. Improvements in actual conditions can still make happiness more robust, and less vulnerable to adversity. It is easier to maintain high levels of well-being and happiness if the conditions are good enough to react adequately. Happiness is a dynamic phenomenon, because it depends on the gratification of needs, but also on perceived gaps between the world as it is and how it should be, in view of demands and expectations. Happiness can go up and down between a minimum and maximum level. It can go up as a result of better conditions and it can go down again due to rising demands and expectations. If progress is interpreted as a linear development, going up all the time and without a maximum, then happiness is unsuitable as a standard. If we use happiness as a standard for progress, then we have to accept that this progress is always between a minimum and maximum. We can always get a more accurate picture by looking at the underlying conditions and the robustness of happiness.

## Weighing and Evaluating the Pros and Cons, a Provisional Value-Free Judgement

The arguments in favour of happiness as a standard, the pros, are quite impressive. The counter-arguments, the cons, are serious, but do not disqualify happiness as a standard. It is clear that it is relatively easy to collect information about evaluative happiness, but we need more information, big data in particular, about affective happiness over longer periods and underlying dynamics. We also need background information about inconsistencies in evaluative happiness. People can easily answer questions about evaluative happiness, but they should get the opportunity to report such inconsistencies. Information about levels of happiness is important and useful, but it is not sufficient.

Unhappiness can indeed be functional and inevitable. That might be a reason to accept it, but it is not an excuse to ignore it. The fact that happiness has a maximum is a useful reminder that we should not try to maximize happiness without any constraints or limits. It is, in particular, a reminder to be critical about commercial advertising. Advertising usually suggests that we can always become happier by spending more money, irrespective of our actual situation and happiness.

The most substantial argument against happiness as a standard is that the relation between happiness and actual living conditions can be illogical, because of adaptation for psychological or strategic reasons. This argument is particularly important since adaptation can function as a camouflage for bad conditions. This counter-argument is convincingly presented by Sen and Nussbaum. Adaptation to bad conditions may never become an excuse for indifference among observers and policy-makers.

It is reassuring that differences in average happiness can be explained quite well by differences in objective living conditions. This explanation is not frustrated or overruled by adaptation or anything else. But the fact that differences in average happiness can be explained by objective realities is no guarantee that there is no adaptation. Adaptation may have a general mitigating impact. The differences in happiness can still be explained by differences in objective conditions, even if the hopelessness of the conditions is not fully expressed in this self-reported happiness.

We may conclude that happiness may never be used as the only standard to assess well-being. We may even be more precise: we should not rely on either subjective or objective standards alone, but try to combine both, to get a more comprehensive picture. Subjective standards can help us to assess the arbitrariness of objective standards, and objective standards can help us to assess the relations between subjective realities like happiness, and actual objective conditions like safety and healthcare. The point that happiness is the most appropriate subjective standard to be used worldwide is obviously important in this context.

There is an important additional argument to apply happiness as a subjective standard in combination with objective standards. We are not only interested in current happiness, but also in future happiness, and therefore in the sustainability and robustness of happiness. The sustainability of happiness, or at least the sustainability of average happiness, depends on the stability and sustainability of living conditions, for example ecological conditions. Combinations of subjective and objective indicators are required to assess and understand current happiness and the sustainability of happiness.

A provisional conclusion is that happiness can be used as a standard but that we have to be careful in its implementation. It is not a panacea and happiness should only be used as a standard in combination with objective standards, to assess well-being and actual and future living conditions. It is important and practical to keep in mind that there are different ways to apply happiness as a standard. It can be applied in a descriptive way to detect and analyse social-economic problems. It can also be applied to set priorities as a starting point for policy developments.

If happiness is used as a standard to be pursued, there are again different possibilities. In the philosophy of classical utilitarianism, happiness should be pursued in a general way, with priority for the most effective options directed at a higher average happiness. In the philosophy of negative utilitarianism, as defended by Popper[8] and Griffin,[9] happiness should be pursued with priority on the reduction of unhappiness and suffering.[10]

The difference is not very dramatic, because in many situations a reduction of unhappiness will be the most effective way to increase average happiness. This is very clear if most people have reached a high level of happiness, and are perhaps close to their maximum. Negative utilitarianism is then the most logical philosophy. Some rich and well-organized high-productivity nations have reached this point. It is dangerous, however, to concentrate on visible unhappiness, because serious unhappiness, for example by anxiety and depression, can be invisible.

It is good to have options! All options are based, however, on the assumption that happiness as a standard, or as an indicator, measure, criterion, norm or goal, is based on happiness as an acceptable and important value. Even the acceptance of happiness as just a descriptive standard would be unjustifiable without this assumption. This assumption deserves some critical attention. We can have a brief look at some alternative values, and at possible tensions between these values and happiness. At this point we have to switch from a value-free approach to a normative approach.

[8] Popper, K. (1945). The open society and its enemies. P.548. Routledge Classics; London and New York.

[9] Griffin, J. (1979). Is unhappiness morally more important than happiness? The Philosophical Quarterly, Vol. 29, no. 114, pp. 47–55. Oxford University Press, on behalf of the Scots Philosophical Association and the University of St. Andrews.

[10] For a discussion of variants of negative utilitarianism see: Arrhenius, G. and Bykvist, K. 1995. *Future Generations and Interpersonal Comparisons: Moral Aspects of Energy Use*. Uppsala: Uppsala Prints and Preprints in Philosophy, nr. 21.

## Happiness and Alternative Values, Some Normative Notions

A famous moral question is whether a surgeon is allowed to sacrifice one patient to use his or her organs, to make some other patients very happy. We might say it is unacceptable, because it creates a lot of unpleasant insecurity for future patients, with a negative impact on happiness in the long term.

We may also argue that happiness is not a dominant value, and that people are, first of all, entitled to some basic rights and minimal respect. I prefer this second solution. Individual rights and minimal respect are dominant and sacrosanct. Formal equality is important in this respect. It means that all individuals have the same rights and duties before the law, and should be treated equally and without discrimination. Minimal respect has a little extra value, because it is also important in informal settings, for example in social contacts between citizens, as in local clubs.

There have been interesting philosophical discussions about the relative priority of happiness. Kant[11] was critical about happiness and put a higher priority on 'doing your duty'. In my view we should be critical about 'doing your duty'. After the work of Kant, at the end of the eighteenth century, there have been many wars and atrocities, by armies with high priorities for hierarchy and duties.

There are more competitors for happiness, but some of them are difficult to define. Solidarity is a very sympathetic value in my view, but the actual content depends very much on specific historic situations. The content of freedom, justice and financial equality is more general and independent of historical situations.

### *Freedom*

Freedom has been discussed in the previous chapter. Just to recapitulate: freedom is the actual individual possibility to choose, and this possibility depends on two dimensions: the opportunity to choose and the individual capability to choose. The opportunity to choose is a characteristic of the environment and depends on the absence of inhibitions and the availability of options. If people think about freedom, they primarily think about

[11] Kant, I.; 1795. Groundwork of the Metaphysics of Morals.

the absence of inhibitions. This absence of inhibitions is occasionally denoted as 'negative freedom'.

The measurement of freedom is usually directed at this negative freedom. The importance of the availability of options and capabilities is usually neglected. Information about options and capabilities in nations can be found in the Human Development Index of the UNDP.[12] This Index, and the underlying statistics, contains a lot of information about purchasing power, life-expectancy and education in nations. Such factors contribute to the availability of options, but also, more in particular, to the development of capabilities.

There are substantial positive correlations between the components of freedom and happiness. We can appreciate freedom, as the actual possibility to choose, in two ways: because freedom contributes to happiness, or for its own sake as an autonomous value. I like both arguments. Freedom is more than just a means to promote well-being. Respect for individual freedom is just an extension of minimal respect and equality before the law. It is unlikely that there will be any substantial tension between freedom and happiness, but it is not impossible. Certain human rights, also the ones related to political rights and civil liberties, are incorporated in national and international legislation. They are fundamental and sacrosanct, and must be protected irrespective of their impact on happiness or anything else.

### *Justice*

Another alternative value or standard is justice, for example as defined by John Rawls. He developed his *justice as fairness*[13] as a system people would approve, if they were behind 'a veil of ignorance', and unaware of their own social-economic position in this system. If people would agree, in such circumstances, about some rules, then such rules should be adopted irrespective of the outcomes. The only condition is that the system may not produce too much inequality in whatever respect. The maximum level of inequality is a level that is still beneficial for everybody. In

[12] http://hdr.undp.org/en/content/human-development-index-hdi

[13] Rawls, J. (1999). A theory of justice, revised edition. Cambridge, MA: Harvard University Press.

this situation it would be in the interest of everybody to accept this inequality, because even the poor would be worse off if this inequality were reduced.

Rawls's proposal is sympathetic as a basic principle, but difficult to apply in practice. Many additional decisions would be needed to specify this theoretical principle. There is however one observation to be made, related to his distinction between 'the rules of the game' and 'the outcomes of the game'.

Rich people have a tendency to put more priority on the status quo and the existing rules of the game. In some nations, like the United States, they may do so because they have the power to adapt the rules to their own interests. Poor people have a tendency to put more priority on the output of the game, for example objective well-being or happiness as subjective well-being. Occasionally they may want to change the rules, to get a better distribution of wealth, income and well-being.

There is no recipe to conclude such discussions. It is obviously important to respect the existing rules and not to change them in some illegal, opportunistic and unpredictable way. It is, on the other hand, also a bridge too far to respect the existing rules by definition, without any regard to actual outcomes. It should be an option to change the rules in a democratic way. In colloquial language we say that the rules of the game should never be changed during the game, but this principle is impractical for a society as a whole, because the game never stops.

Existing rules must be respected if they are the results of decent and democratic procedures. From empirical research we know that there is a strong positive correlation between happiness and the quality of such rules, not just on paper and in the books, but also in practice. This practice is expressed in Rule of Law, as one of the aspects of the Delivery Quality of governments. The high correlation with happiness is understandable, since people and organizations need some stability and predictability, in order to be able to make plans and carry them out.

Existing rules must be respected, but the consequences of the rules, or the output, should be assessed regularly. This can be done by anybody, for example politicians, policy-makers or other individuals, or by any organization with some interest, for example the media, research institutes, government agencies, political parties, trade unions, employers and consumer associations. Individuals and organizations can apply whatever standard they prefer. They can apply inequality as a standard, as suggested by Rawls, but also objective well-being, or subjective well-being such as happiness.

We may conclude that stability and predictability of rules are important for happiness, but happiness can also be used as a standard to assess the consequences of the rules. If rules do not contribute to happiness, they may be changed, but only in a democratic way with respect for reasonable expectations and established interests. This conclusion is consistent with the vision of Jeremy Bentham that happiness can be used as a standard to assess the consequences of intended legislation.[14]

## *Financial Inequality*

Some people want more than formal equality before the law and minimal respect. They want full equality in more respects, for example in income and wealth. Such demands are ambitious and can be problematic for happiness, and also for justice and freedom. Differences in wealth and income depend a great deal on fundamental personal characteristics that cannot be changed or compensated for, for example differences in genes, personality, objective health and creativity.

It is, on the other hand, unfortunate that in many societies inequality is really grotesque and beyond any justification. The United States is a clear example. As observed by Wolff[15] and reported by Stiglitz:[16] in 2007 1% of the households controlled 35% of national wealth, and 40% if the value of homes is excluded. This inequality goes together with serious poverty for substantial minorities, and it contributes to aggression, anxiety and depression. Such inequality is also a serious threat to the principles of formal equality before the law and minimal respect. There is obviously a serious conflict between this inequality and happiness.

This inequality has also a disruptive impact on the functioning of political systems. Rich people and organizations have enough financial power to mislead people and to change or maintain the existing rules and policies, just to defend their private interests.[17] Such developments have a negative

[14] Bentham, J. (1789). The Principles of Morals and Legislation.

[15] Wolff, E. (2010). Recent trends in household wealth in the United States: rising debt and the middle-class squeeze- an update to 2007. Levy Institute, Working paper no. 589, March 2010.

[16] Stiglitz, J. (2012). The price of inequality. W.W. Norton & Company. New York (Page 2).

[17] It is symptomatic to see how people in the United States are deceived with complicated financial products, without any serious countervailing power of the government or the judiciary.

impact on general trust and this may have serious consequences. As pointed out by Rothstein and Uslaner,[18] there is an interdependency between equality, good governance and trust. In a negative scenario nations can get locked up in a paralysing inequality trap, by this interdependency. This is apparently what has happened in the United States, and in many other nations: extreme inequality leads to a low level of social trust and ineffective governance. As a consequence the inequality is beyond repair.

There are nevertheless possibilities to get out of the trap. The interdependencies are not complete. Inequality can be reduced by trade unions and other non-government organizations, independently of government and trust. The quality of government can be improved in a technical way, independently of inequality and trust. Trust can be improved by solidarity and more priority for the interests of the poor, independently of inequality and government.

There is also a bright spot to be noticed. In some nations, like the Scandinavian nations, we see simultaneously combinations of high average happiness, equality in happiness and substantial financial inequality in terms of wealth[19] and income. The explanation is that many important facilities, like safety, healthcare and education, have become available for everybody, irrespective of their financial resources. In this situation there is still a minimum 'level playing field' for children, irrespective of the financial situation of their parents. This disconnection of money and happiness is an interesting recipe for more happiness. It is an acceptable reason to be lenient about financial inequality, as long as the impact on happiness is modest.

We may conclude that there is a strong relation between unjustifiable inequality and unhappiness. Such inequality is also inconsistent with the Rawls's principle that inequality should be beneficial for the poor. A reduction of inequality, or a disconnection of financial inequality and happiness, would be a big step in the direction of more happiness and well-being.

[18] Rothstein, B., & Uslaner, E.M. (2005). All for all: Equality, corruption, and social trust. World Politics, 58 (1), 41–72.

[19] Piketty, T. (2013). Capital in the Twenty-First Century. Éditions du Seuil; Harvard University Press.

## Conclusions

We can use happiness as a subjective standard in combination with objective standards to assess well-being. It is highly valued and it is easy to collect information about evaluative happiness.

There are some serious complications. It is not a panacea. Even with happiness as a standard there are still many decisions to be made about priorities. Happiness as a standard is not a substitute for personal and political deliberations and discussions.

The relations between happiness and actual living conditions can be illogical, even if the differences in average happiness can be explained by differences in such conditions. It is therefore essential to combine happiness as a subjective standard with objective standards, in order to assess the relation between happiness and actual conditions.

There are, arguably, no systematic tensions between happiness as a value and alternative values, like equality before the law, minimal respect, freedom, justice and some minimal financial equality. It is possible, however, that there are tensions in specific situations. It is important, in such situations, to accept that there are alternative standards, based on alternative values that should be respected, irrespective of the relation with happiness.

Happiness can be used as a standard in different ways. It can be used in a modest way as a descriptive standard to collect and analyse information about well-being. It can also be used in a more ambitious way as a standard to be pursued, and as a standard to decide about policies and priorities. It is wise, in view of the complications just mentioned, to use happiness primarily in a modest way, to collect and analyse information. This information, and the results of the analysis, can be used as input in personal and political deliberations. Perhaps it can be used occasionally to decide about priorities, but never in some automatic or self-evident way.

Happiness might get more attention if it is used as a standard, even if it is only used in a modest way. More attention might facilitate a development towards more appreciation, and a somewhat higher relative priority for happiness as a value. In my view this is acceptable. This view is based on the inventory of pros and cons, but also on my expectation that a somewhat higher priority for happiness will not have a negative impact on the importance of the alternative values just mentioned: equality before the law, minimal respect, individual freedom, justice and some minimal financial equality. However, in my view it would be acceptable if it had a negative effect on the relative importance of utility-based values, like maximal economic growth, personal income, profits and employment in terms of paid jobs. But this is a personal/political conviction about how the world ought to be, and this conviction is obviously not value-free.

In the next chapter we can specify how happiness can be used as a standard in personal life and in politics. We may also use our imagination to carry out some 'What if' exercises, to find out what the consequences might be of a somewhat higher priority for happiness as a value.

CHAPTER 9

# What If? A More Critical Lifestyle and Some Policy Options

## Happiness as a Standard in Our Personal Life

What could we expect if individuals were to accept happiness more deliberately as a descriptive standard and/or as a standard to be pursued in their personal life? It can be argued that it would not change their life dramatically. People already think a lot about their appreciation of life, for good reasons. It is convenient, because a comprehensive appreciation can facilitate quick decisions, if there are new opportunities or problems. A comprehensive appreciation can also be functional for psychological or strategic reasons. And last but not least: the evaluation of life is an interesting issue to be discussed with partners, relatives and friends.

People may think a lot about their happiness, but unfortunately they usually do not adopt or adapt the standards they apply deliberately, or even knowingly. Usually they just adopt or internalize popular standards in their social environment. This is regrettable, because it makes them vulnerable to cognitive peculiarities and social dynamics like manipulation, social comparison and positional competition. Combinations of cognitive peculiarities and social dynamics may have a negative impact on happiness.

If people accept happiness as a standard more deliberately in their personal life, we may expect them to become more critical about the standards they apply, or have applied, in the evaluation of their life. We may also expect that they will be more critical if they adapt standards or adopt


J. Ott, *Beyond Economics*,
https://doi.org/10.1007/978-3-030-56600-5_9

new ones. Perhaps they will also pay more attention to the inconsistencies in their evaluative happiness, and find solutions.

It is a bit unfortunate, however, that the explanation of differences in individual happiness within nations is problematic. Some reasons, just to recapitulate:

(a) The differences are small, particularly in nations with a high average.
(b) There are regular and irregular fluctuations in individual happiness.
(c) The available information is insufficient, in particular about affective happiness in childhood and mental problems. More information is also required about the impact of individual genetics.
(d) A more fundamental reason might be that the qualitative comparability of individual happiness is limited, because there is too much diversity and indeterminacy in standards to develop general explanations. This diversity and indeterminacy can be products of more individual freedom in high-productivity nations.

There are many interesting publications about happiness and well-being, in particular in nations with a high average happiness, but the inconvenient truth is that the currently available knowledge is not good enough to explain the differences in individual happiness. It would be premature, however, to conclude that it is useless for people to adopt happiness as a standard to be pursued in their personal life.

The lack of general knowledge can be compensated for by a more profound knowledge of personal needs and ambitions. It is a plausible expectation that personal deliberations and discussions about well-being will become more effective and productive. We may also expect that people will pay more attention to the subjective and objective well-being of other people. Perhaps they will even change their lifestyle.[1]

People will learn that they have substantial freedom to accept new challenges, as soon as they understand that their fundamental needs are gratified and will be gratified in the future. Rich and happy retired people in high-productivity nations are already in this situation. Making unhappy people happy might be an interesting challenge.

[1] Some (well-known) options: they can buy correct 'fair-trade' products and reject conspicuous consumption, for example no more flowers from Africa and no more long-distance flying for short fun. People can reflect upon eating less meat, donate more money to charity and can put a higher priority on social relations. They can work as volunteers and care for people with some handicap or illness.

## Happiness as a Standard in Politics

What would happen if happiness became a popular descriptive standard and/or a standard to be pursued in politics, to be applied in combination with objective standards? There is a substantial amount of knowledge about factors that affect average happiness in nations. This knowledge can be used, and further developed. The quality of government is a crucial factor, and this quality can be improved. It is certainly not a vague or 'wicked' concept.

It is still unusual, however, to accept happiness as a standard in politics. There is attention to objective well-being, for example in terms of health and utility-based standards, and there is attention to political preferences, for example preferences for policy options and existing political parties. It is difficult to predict what would happen if evaluative happiness became more popular as an additional standard. We may speculate, however, that it might contribute to a better and more comprehensive understanding of subjective and objective well-being and their mutual relations. We may also speculate that there will be more attention to visible and less visible unhappiness.

Evaluative happiness is also an interesting issue for politicians, policy-makers and political scientists. Information about evaluative happiness can help them to understand political preferences and the results of elections. It is a reasonable expectation that political deliberations and discussions about subjective and objective well-being will become more effective.

There are other positive consequences, even if happiness is only used as a descriptive standard. With happiness as a descriptive standard, it will be possible to detect unhappiness and to identify and analyse the related problems. Such information would at least facilitate a reduction of visible and less visible unhappiness and suffering, as promulgated in the philosophy of negative utilitarianism. We may expect, however, that a reduction of unhappiness will have beneficial side-effects for all citizens, due to a reduction of negative feelings like insecurity and anxiety. A less obvious consequence might be that national governments will put a higher priority on the interests of nations with a low average happiness, for example in their international trade relations.

In a nutshell: more attention to happiness, as a standard in politics, may lead to more attention to unhappy people, either as minorities in happy nations or as majorities in less happy nations. In rich nations this higher priority may lead to less priority for utility-based indicators, used to assess national living conditions.

Rich nations have many options to reduce the unhappiness of their own minorities, and the unhappiness of majorities in less productive nations. There are also options to make the happiness of happy people more robust and less vulnerable to adversity, such as a pandemic. In the first introductory chapter some problems of neo-liberalism, related to happiness and objective well-being, were mentioned. In the following paragraphs some policies are suggested to manage these problems, if happiness is used as a standard. These policies are presented to stimulate our imagination.

## A. In General: More Priority for Fundamental Needs in Poor Nations

The most general problem with neo-liberalism is that the gratification of needs just depends on the availability of money. The gratification of marginal needs, like the need for challenges and conspicuous consumption, gets the same priority as the gratification of fundamental needs, like the need for safety and security. The implication is that marginal needs of rich people will be gratified, while fundamental needs of the poor will not be gratified. This problem has a negative impact on happiness, particularly in poor nations. The low levels of average happiness in poor nations are dramatic. There is no excuse for ignoring these low levels. The interests of poor nations with a low level of average happiness deserve a higher priority.

According to the neo-liberal ideology, governments are not supposed to promote the interests of specific private enterprises. But the reality is very different. Governments of rich nations work together with their business people and are very effective in protecting their national commercial interests. The governments of poor nations do not have the same information, expertise and power to act accordingly.

## B. Less Positional Competition Through a Better Organization of Security

In most rich countries there is insurance, for example, for medical care, and there are collective provisions to create some financial security. The levels of such insurance and provisions are usually not high enough.

A strong financial position is still needed to create financial security, at great age or earlier. People have to save money before they get old and vulnerable.

This organization of security is inefficient. Usually people will save more than they need. A more fundamental disadvantage is that they have to earn money as long as they possibly can. This situation creates positional competition, for example, for jobs, with an upward pressure to produce paid commodities and services. This upward pressure has a negative impact on sustainability, on individual freedom and on the distribution of work.

Security should be organized in a cheaper and more effective way. There are—at least—three policies for doing so. It is possible to provide for high levels of collective provisions, available irrespective of income or wealth. The other policies are a basic income or a negative income tax.[2] It is probably wise to combine such policies, since all of them have their specific pros and cons.

Such policies reduce the need for positional competition and improve social security, but can contribute to happiness in more ways. They can facilitate voluntary work and reduce financial insecurity and the risk of exploitation, because people will have more freedom to reject jobs if the conditions are unacceptable. The policies would also reduce the vulnerability of the economy to the financial consequences of epidemic or pandemic diseases.[3]

For many people positional competition will always be an appealing challenge, but for other people it will be more attractive to accept a productive but more relaxed lifestyle. It is good to have options!

[2] The options of a basic income or a negative income tax, and high levels of collective provisions, available irrespective of income or wealth, can be combined in many ways. All options reduce the impact of a low household income on well-being and happiness. See also: Friedman, M. Capitalism and Freedom (1962). University of Chicago Press.

[3] The economic problems by the Coronavirus in 2020 are a clear example: a lot of financial misery and a terrible recession caused by a strong reduction of effective demand. A basic income or a negative income tax, and a high level of collective provisions, would make it easier to handle such situations.

## c. Less Upward Pressure on Production and Consumption, More Individual Freedom

The upward pressure to produce and consume is clearly expressed in the permanent overdose of commercial advertising people have to endure every day. This advertising has a negative impact on the individual freedom to adopt and adapt standards for the evaluation of life. A more specific negative effect is that people are pushed to spend more money, and to put a lower priority on activities which do not involve expenditure, like social contacts, social activities or work as a volunteer.

Advertisers always try to create perceptions of gaps between *is* and *ought*, in such a way that people go shopping, and they do so by the exploitation of cognitive peculiarities and social dynamics, like social comparison. The practical usefulness of commercials is usually very limited, since people are permanently exposed to commercials, even in periods when they are not at all interested in buying the recommended commodities or services.[4]

Commercial advertising has become a very dominant type of manipulation in neo-liberal societies. It would obviously be wrong and unjustifiable to forbid commercial advertising. Advertising can be useful and entertaining. The correct approach is giving people real opportunities to decide what kind of advertising they want to be exposed to, if any. It is easy to create such freedom for people who watch TV, listen to the radio or are on the internet. Politicians should take this up together with advertisers and internet service providers.

The practical value of advertising would be more substantial if people were free to decide to be exposed to it or not. It is first of all a matter of decency, however, to develop such possibilities. Many advertisers would appreciate such interventions, because they prefer communication based on free choice. Most of them do not want to brainwash anyone, or to push their messages down anyone's throat.

[4] No data available, but my estimation is that in the Netherlands people get exposed to commercials about cars on average 2 minutes per day, 15 minutes per week or 1 hour per month. But most of them do not buy cars, and if they do, it will be once in about every five years.

## D. More Priority for Ecological Sustainability and Sustainability of Happiness

The upward pressure to produce and consume also has a negative impact on ecological sustainability and the sustainability of happiness. In some nations the numbers of inhabitants and quantity of houses and infrastructure are getting close to the physical limits in terms of space, biodiversity and sustainability. In a nation like the Netherlands this is very visible. Green spots disappear, biodiversity is deteriorating rapidly and the country is becoming more vulnerable to epidemics, drought and floods.

This vulnerability became clear in the Corona epidemic in 2020. A limited lock-down created a run on parks and beaches, and there were more infections in regions with a high population density. A high population density, with a lack of green spaces, is a very negative factor in such situations. We may say that our freedom and happiness are in danger, if we are unable to stop these developments.

One thing is very clear and undeniable: we can continue to replace old buildings and infrastructure that have reached the end of their useful life, but someday we have to stop taking over more land for human use. The only questions are: when, and how do we prepare for it? A discussion about such issues would be a useful exercise.

## E. Better Distribution of Labour in High-Productivity Nations

Another problem, mentioned in the introductory chapter, is the distribution of labour in high-productivity-nations. Differences in levels of income have become less effective as motivating factors. This is a good thing in itself, but it creates nasty problems. In rich nations like the Netherlands it makes it difficult to find people who want to take care of vulnerable young or old people, or people with some disability.

The policy of central banks, to pump cheap money into the economy, is in fact an effort to solve such problems, but it is not effective. It is a random and crude approach, without any selectivity. It leads to low interest rates, with negative consequences for pensions. It also creates more financial inequality, since rich people and their banks, bad banks included, benefit disproportionally. Banks get the cheap money first, and can make substantial profits if they lend it out again.[5] The central banks pass the money on to private banks, hoping they will somehow activate and motivate consumers and entrepreneurs to do sensible things.

A better understanding of the pursuit of happiness, as an alternative motivating factor, can make it easier to get the work done, without such kill or cure remedies. It would help if alternative mechanisms to allocate paid and unpaid work played a more substantial role. In many societies we already see a rise in voluntary work, in particular among healthy retired people. Such volunteers do not work for money but for different reasons. They just like the work as such, or the associated social relations, or they see their work as a personal challenge or as a social obligation. Perhaps we may say that the money economy has reached its limits and that we should go back a few steps, and put more priority on the social distribution of work.

## F. Selective Social Policies

Unemployment and financial insecurity have a negative impact on happiness.[6] Usually unemployed people are pushed in the same way to apply for paid jobs. No distinction is made between people who really suffer as a result of their unemployment, and people who do not suffer, for example, because they make other people happy as volunteers.

It would be wise to pay more attention to people who really suffer, and less attention to people who are happy and contribute to the happiness of others. It would even be wise to cancel the usual obligation to apply for paid work for volunteers. The social-economic damage of unemployment, in terms of happiness, would be substantially reduced by more selective policies.

[5] Stiglitz, J. (2012). The price of inequality. W.W. Norton & Company. New York (Page 245). "If a bank can borrow at close to zero, and buy a long-term government bond yielding, say 3 percent, it makes a nifty 3 percent profit for doing nothing. Lend the banking system a trillion dollars a year, and that's a $30 billion gift. But banks can often do better…."

[6] Ott, J. (2015) Impact of Size and Quality of Governments on Happiness: Financial Insecurity as a Key-Problem in Market-Democracies. Journal of Happiness Studies, Vol. 16, nr. 6. pp. 1639–1647.

## Conclusion

The adoption of happiness as a standard in our personal life and in politics may have some interesting positive consequences. The presentation of some policy options, to be considered if happiness were adopted as a standard, may stimulate our imagination.

## Bibliography

Friedman, M. (1962). *Capitalism and freedom*. Chicago, IL: University of Chicago Press.

Ott, J. (2015). Impact of size and quality of governments on happiness: Financial insecurity as a key-problem in market-democracies. *Journal of Happiness Studies, 16*(6), 1639–1647.

Stiglitz, J. (2012). *The price of inequality*. New York: W.W. Norton & Company.

CHAPTER 10

# Summary, Concluding Remarks and General Conclusion

## Summary

There has been, and still is, a lot of confusion about happiness. The confusion can be reduced by accepting the definition of happiness as the enduring appreciation of life as a whole. The implication is that happiness is not about being happy about something specific, it is not about some perfect state, it is not about utility, and happiness is not by definition egocentric, altruistic or morally acceptable.

The confusion can be further reduced by the results of empirical research. Positive and negative emotions, as the elements of affective or 'experiential happiness', have their own dynamics. Another result is that people answer in a rather cognitive way, if questions are asked about their overall happiness. As a consequence the usual typology of happiness, with affective, cognitive and overall happiness, can be transformed into a typology with positive emotions, negative emotions and evaluative happiness based on adopted standards. If positive and negative emotions are taken together as the elements of affective happiness, then we may even apply a simple dichotomy: affective and evaluative happiness.

A key finding in happiness research is that people worldwide think a lot about their appreciation of their own life as a whole. It is convenient to have such a general appreciation, also for psychological and strategic reasons. It is possible, however, that people come up with a general appreciation but ignore certain inconsistencies, for example, between emotions


J. Ott, *Beyond Economics*,
https://doi.org/10.1007/978-3-030-56600-5_10

and cognitive evaluation or between the standards they apply in their evaluation of life.

The fact that people think a lot about their own happiness makes it rather easy to measure evaluative happiness, based on some thinking or reflection. The measurement of affective happiness, or positive and negative emotions, is made more complicated by regular and irregular fluctuations. Evaluative happiness is the most convenient type of happiness to analyse and to work with.

It would be a mistake, however, to assume that emotions are irrelevant for evaluative happiness. Emotions over longer periods and in childhood have eventually a strong cumulative impact on personal development and evaluative happiness. We may even assume that an evaluation of life as a whole, without any emotions, is futile and almost meaningless.

Affective happiness, with positive and negative emotions as elements, depends a great deal on the gratification of needs. It is a bridge too far to assume that, in the terminology of Maslow, the gratification of 'lower' needs in his pyramid is a condition for the gratification of 'higher' needs.

It is plausible, however, that the gratification of some lower needs has more impact on happiness over the life-course than the gratification of higher needs. Frustration of the lower needs for safety and security by bad conditions in childhood may have a very negative cumulative impact on evaluative happiness. If happiness is accepted as a standard then it is justifiable to argue that the gratification of the fundamental needs, for safety and security, deserves a higher priority than the gratification of other needs.

People adopt and adapt standards for appreciating or evaluating their life. Unfortunately, but inevitably, they usually do this unknowingly. The adoption and adaptation of standard is therefore subject to cognitive peculiarities and social dynamics, like social comparison, manipulation and positional competition.

It is relatively easy to explain differences in average evaluative happiness in nations, using four explanatory factors related to objective realities: GDP per capita, safety and security as reflected in healthy life expectancy, and the Democratic and Delivery Quality of government. This is an indication that the comparability of average happiness in nations, possibly with different cultures, is good. Apparently people in different nations adopt the same or at least similar standards to appreciate their life.

It is difficult to explain individual differences in evaluative happiness within nations. This might be a consequence of a lack of information about individual differences in genetic and personality characteristics, emotional development and mental problems. However, there might be an alternative reason for the ineffectiveness of the explanations: perhaps there is a lack of comparability because of diversity in the standards individuals within a nation apply in their evaluation of life. Time will tell what will happen if more information about individual characteristics can be used.

The quality of government is an important factor for average happiness in nations. This quality is important in direct contacts between government agencies and citizens, and for the creation and maintenance of conditions that facilitate the pursuit of happiness.

The relation between governments and citizens is a sensitive issue. Governments have to be very accurate in the application of the general rules for good governance and in respecting the separation of the three powers: legislative, executive and judicial power. They must also be clear and transparent about their ambitions, in order to avoid confusion about responsibilities.

There are arguments in favour of happiness as a standard and there are arguments against happiness as a standard. Happiness can be useful as a general standard in a globalizing world, and perhaps it can compensate for shortcomings in human empathy. Taking all arguments together it is possible to accept happiness as a standard, but with some annotations. Happiness as a standard should not be exclusively directed at levels of happiness, but also at the consistency and the robustness or vulnerability of happiness. It should be used in combination with objective standards, concerning the quality of actual living conditions. This is important because the relation between happiness and actual conditions can be illogical, for example, because happiness has a maximum or as a result of adaptation. Objective standards can help us to assess the potential impact of adaptation and to assess the robustness or vulnerability of happiness.

Happiness can be used as a standard in different ways. It can be used as just a descriptive standard to identify problems and to analyse such problems, but it can also be used as a standard to be pursued, and to set priorities. It is wise to start with happiness as a descriptive standard, and to use it in a more ambitious way in specific situations and contexts.

If happiness is used as a descriptive standard, it will be convenient to concentrate on evaluative happiness, because it is easier to collect comparable information about evaluative happiness anywhere in the world, for example with the ladder scale. A more fundamental argument is that evaluative happiness is based on the standards people have adopted themselves. Affective happiness, and in particular long-term affective happiness, is important and integrated into evaluative happiness, but people may put different priorities on positive and negative emotions, as the elements of affective happiness.

If happiness is used as a standard to be pursued, there are again different possibilities. In the philosophy of classical utilitarianism, happiness should be pursued in a general way, with priority for the most effective ways of creating more happiness. The efforts will be directed at a higher average happiness in whatever way. In the philosophy of negative utilitarianism, the reduction of unhappiness and suffering takes priority over maximizing total happiness.

The difference is not very dramatic, because in many situations a reduction of unhappiness will be the most effective way to increase average happiness. The difference may even be negligible if many people in a society have reached a high level of happiness, and are perhaps close to their maximum. In such situations a reduction of unhappiness is obviously the most appropriate approach in both philosophies. Some rich and well-organized high-productivity nations have reached such situations. The argument that the most visible unhappiness should get the highest priority is somewhat dangerous, since serious unhappiness can be invisible, for example, if people are suffering from a depression.

If happiness is accepted as a standard in our personal life, it might help us to become more critical about the standards we have adopted and the adoption of new standards. This can contribute to more effective personal deliberations and discussions about happiness. It is a handicap that the explanation of individual differences within nations is not effective, but up to a point we can compensate for this lack of general knowledge by a more comprehensive and profound knowledge of our own needs, preferences and ambitions.

If happiness is accepted as a standard in politics, some problems of neo-liberalism will be given more attention, like the gratification of fundamental needs of the poor and the upward pressure on production and consumption, with a negative impact on individual freedom and ecological sustainability.

## Concluding Remarks

### *Terminology: To Be Practical*

It is acceptable to distinguish just affective and evaluative happiness, but with some annotations.

(a) It can be important to distinguish negative and positive emotions as elements in affective happiness, because they have their own dynamics.
(b) It is important to distinguish short- and long-term affective happiness because the interaction between long-term affective happiness and evaluative happiness is more important than the interaction between short-term affective happiness and evaluative happiness.
(c) Evaluative happiness is an outcome of some reflection or cognitive activity. It is based on the adoption of standards. Affective happiness, or the hedonic level of affect, is always one of the standards. For children and for people with a cognitive handicap, it may even be the only or dominant standard. Adults adopt more standards.
(d) Evaluative happiness is a better starting point to assess subjective well-being, since it is based on the standards adopted by the people themselves.

### *Individual Freedom and Happiness*

The most fundamental source of confusion about happiness is that people are free to adopt and adapt their own standards. In theory this may create four types of problems.

(a) People may adopt very inconsistent standards; this might make their own individual happiness inconsistent and possibly instable.
(b) They may adopt very different standards; this may lead to incomparability of happiness of different individuals.
(c) They may change their standards frequently; this may lead to instability of happiness.
(d) The standards people adopt can be immoral, or to formulate this more precisely, standards can be immoral if compared with alternative standards, based on a different morality, with different values, for example, related to equality or gender and racial relations.

In reality people usually adopt consistent and similar standards and do not change them too often. The standards are morally acceptable in general, as reflected in the fact that happy people are usually good citizens.[1] But there are exceptions and we have to be critical. We also have to keep in mind that people usually adopt similar standards, but not necessarily with the same priorities, for example for positive and negative emotions.

## *Happiness: Collective or Individual?*

It is possible to explain the dramatic differences in average happiness in nations effectively, by four factors related to objective realities: GDP per capita, safety and security as reflected in healthy life expectancy, and the Democratic and Delivery Quality of government. Such collective conditions play a crucial role in average happiness.

It is difficult to explain individual differences within nations.[2] One reason is that there is a lack of simple but representative information about long-term affective happiness, related to emotional experiences, mental problems, personality and genetics. More information, possibly to be collected in surveys and panel studies, is needed to assess the importance of individual differences. We may assume that certain differences, for example in physical and mental health, in personality characteristics and in social-economic status, are important.

Perhaps it is also difficult to explain differences in individual happiness, if the differences are small and if there is more freedom in the adoption of standards. This individual freedom can lead to more indeterminacy and a lack of comparability.

[1] See footnote 2 in Chap. 8: Guven, C. (2011). Are happier people better citizens? Kyklos, 64 (2), 178–192.

[2] This is a very general conclusion. There are a lot of research results about the importance of specific conditions. We know that the impact of unemployment or losing a spouse is very negative. We know that there is a positive correlation between happiness and being married or having a partner. We also know that there is a u-shape in the relation between age and happiness: people are less happy in their middle ages, possibly due to an overload of obligations like making money, finding and keeping a partner, taking care of children and parents. Such results are interesting and important, but we have to be careful. As long as we can only explain and understand a small portion of observed differences in happiness, then we do not really know what is going on.

It will always be questionable to compare the impact of collective and individual conditions on happiness. Collective conditions in nations are obviously useless in the explanation of individual differences in happiness within nations, because they are identical for all citizens. Theoretically it is an option to try to explain the happiness of individuals living in different nations, with their nationality as one of the explanatory factors. This is contentious, however, since the interaction between collective and individual factors is too intense and complicated to disentangle their impact.

It is important to pay attention to the composition of samples used in research, in order to interpret the conclusions correctly. One example: we may read in the newspapers that genetics explain a substantial portion of happiness differences. If the sample is composed of individuals living in one nation, then we must realize that the common conditions in the nation are left out. This is not unusual, but the implication is that the role of individual differences is frequently overestimated, by omitting national collective conditions.

### *Clarity About Happiness Contributes to Effective Deliberations and Discussions*

It is always good to reduce confusion, but there are additional reasons to reduce confusion about happiness. Happiness is a specific type of subjective well-being, and well-being is an important subject in many personal and political deliberations and discussions. A reduction of confusion can make the deliberations and discussions more effective, and it may even have a positive effect on the functioning of political systems.

Some political systems contribute more to happiness than others, through characteristics like a parliamentary executive, a proportional representation electoral system, as opposed to single-member districts, and a unitary governmental structure.[3] Such characteristics probably have a moderating impact on polarization and a positive impact on political deliberations and discussions. Such deliberations and discussions can be further improved by reducing confusion about happiness and well-being.

[3] See footnote 13 in Chap. 7: Altman, D.; Flavin, P.; Radcliff, B.F.; (2016). Democratic Institutions and Subjective Well-Being. Political Studies, 2016, 1–20.

### *Happiness as a Standard Facilitates Critical Analysis of Neo-liberalism*

The application of happiness as a standard makes it easier to define the shortcomings of neo-liberalism more accurately. Neo-liberalism has fundamental advantages, but there are some unacceptable problems resulting from the way it is currently organized.

It is interesting to notice that one problematic characteristic of neo-liberalism is very basic, and a starting point for some other problems: the strong relation between personal income and the production of goods and services.

This strong relation works well if there is scarcity of goods and services, but it creates problems if labour productivity is high enough to put an end to scarcity. If income and work are not disconnected when labour productivity is high, individuals are compelled to produce whatever it takes to gratify the marginal needs of the rich. Even new needs will have to be invented occasionally, like nail studios for cats and dogs, meditation courses, surgical interventions to improve appearance and legal help to fight out personal injuries.

There is nothing wrong with such needs or the gratification of such needs, and we should never become paternalistic about their legitimacy. But it is clear that the gratification of some needs contributes more to happiness over the course of life than the gratification of others. If we qualify these needs as fundamental and less fundamental, respectively, and if we adopt happiness as a standard to be pursued, then we may conclude that the gratification of fundamental needs deserves a higher priority.

## General Conclusion

Perhaps it is not a very spectacular step to accept happiness as a descriptive standard and/or as a standard to be pursued in our personal life or in politics, but we may expect some positive consequences.

Happiness as a standard in our personal life can help us to be more critical about the standards we have adopted, or want to adopt, to appreciate our life as a whole. It can stimulate us to be apprehensive about our own happiness and about happiness or unhappiness in our social environment. It can also help us to decide about our lifestyle and political preferences.

Happiness as a standard in politics can help us to identify and analyse unhappiness and the sustainability of happiness more effectively, in our own nation or elsewhere. Perhaps it can even help us to set priorities in politics, but this is not self-evident and can never happen in some automatic or self-evident way. Happiness as a standard can never be a substitute for politics, but happiness research can produce relevant information as input for politics.

The most general positive effect of happiness as a standard is that it may have a positive impact on the effectiveness of personal and political deliberations and discussions, about subjective and objective well-being.

## Bibliography

Altman, D., Flavin, P., & Radcliff, B. F. (2016). Democratic institutions and subjective well-being. *Political Studies, 2016*, 1–20.

Guven, C. (2011). Are happier people better citizens? *Kyklos, 64*(2), 178–192.

# Bibliography; Beyond Economics: Happiness as a Standard in our Personal Life and in Politics; J.C. Ott

Abrams, M., Gerard, T., & Timms, N. (1985). *Values and social change in Britain*. London: Macmillan.
Alexandrova, A. (2017). *A philosophy for the science of well-being*. Oxford: Oxford University Press.
Altman, D., Flavin, P., & Radcliff, B. F. (2016). Democratic institutions and subjective well-being. *Political Studies, 2016*, 1–20.
Arrhenius, G., & Bykvist, K. (1995). *Future generations and interpersonal comparisons: Moral aspects of energy use*. Uppsala: Uppsala Prints and Preprints in Philosophy, nr. 21.
Bache, I., & Reardon, L. (2016). *The politics and policy of wellbeing*. Cheltenham: Edward Elgar Publishing.
Bartolini, S., Bilancini, B., Bruni, L., & Porta, P. L. (Eds.). (2016). *Policies for happiness*. Oxford: Oxford University Press.
Bay, C. (1958). *The structure of freedom*. Stanford, CA: Stanford University Press.
Bentham, J. (1789). *The theory of morals and legislation*.
Bergsma, A. (1995). *Emoties en kwaliteit van bestaan [Emotions and quality of life]*. Utrecht: Het Spectrum.
Berlin, I. (1958). Two concepts of liberty. In Berlin (author) and Hardy (Ed.), (2002) *Liberty: Incorporating four essays on liberty*. Oxford: Oxford University Press.
Boom, P. (2013). *Just babies. The origins of good and evil*. New York: Crown Publishers.
Bradburn, N. M. (1969). *The structure of psychological well-being*. Chicago: Aldine.


J. Ott, *Beyond Economics*,
https://doi.org/10.1007/978-3-030-56600-5

Brickman, P., & Campbell, D. T. (1971). Hedonic relativism and planning the good society. In M. H. Appley (Ed.), *Adaptation level theory: A symposium* (pp. 287–302). New York: Academic Press.

Buijs, P. (2007). *The age of happiness. Dutch opinions on happiness during the enlightenment, 1658–1835.* Dissertation, Utrecht, with a summary in English.

Cantril, H. (1965). *The pattern of human concerns.* New York: New Brunswick.

Clark, A., et al. (2018). *The origins of happiness.* Princeton & Oxford: Princeton University Press.

Condorcet, N. (1785). Essay on the application of analysis to the probability of majority decisions.

Conway, A., et al. (2013). The broaden-and-build theory of positive emotions: Form, function, and mechanisms. In S. David, I. Boniwell, & A. Conley Ayers (Eds.), *The oxford handbook of happiness.* Oxford: Oxford University Press.

Csikzentmihalyi, M., & Hunter, J. (2003). The use of experience sampling. *Journal of Happiness Studies, 4*(2), 185–199.

Cummins, R. A. (2010). Subjective wellbeing, homeostatically protected mood and depression: A synthesis. *Journal of Happiness Studies, 11*(1), 1–17.

Dalkey, N. C. (1973). *Studies in the quality of life.* Lexington: Lexington Books.

Damasio, A. (1994). *Descartes' error, emotions, reason and the human brain.* New York: Harper Perennial.

de La Mettrie, J. O. (1748). *L'Homme Machine.*

Descartes, R. (1641). *Meditationes de Prima Philosophia.* Descartes (1644). Principia Philosophia.

Diener, E. (1994). Assessing subjective well-being: Progress and opportunities. *Social Indicators Research, 31*, 103–157.

Diener, E., & Emmons, R. (1984). The independence of positive and negative affect. *Journal of Personality and Social Psychology, 47*, 1105–1117.

Diener, E., Larsen, L. J., Levine, S., & Emmons, R. A. (1985). Intensity and frequency: Dimensions underlying positive and negative affect. *Journal of Personality and Social Psychology, 48*, 1253–1265.

Diener, E., Lucas, R., & Scollon, C. N. (2006). Beyond the hedonic treadmill: Revisiting the adaptation theory of well-being. *American Psychologist, 61*(4), 305–314.

Dolan, P. (2014). *Happiness by design.* New York: Penguin Group.

Easterlin, R. (1974). Does economic growth improve the human lot? Some empirical evidence. In P. A. David & W. Reder (Eds.), *Nations and households in economic growth: Essays in honour of Moses Abramowitz.* New York: Academic Press.

Ehrhardt, J., Veenhoven, R., & Saris, W. (2000). Stability of life-satisfaction over time. Analysis of change in ranks in a national population. *Journal of Happiness Studies, 1*, 177–205.

Elchardus, M., & Smits, W. (2007). *Het Grootste Geluk.* Leuven: LannooCampus.

Emmons, R., & Diener, E. (1985). Personality correlates of subjective well-being. *Journal of Personality and Social Psychology, 11*, 89–97.

Etzioni, A. (2018). *Happiness is the wrong metric; a liberal communitarian response to populism (dedicated to the moral wrestlers)*. Washington, DC: The George Washington University.

Fleurbaey, M., & Blanchet, D. (2013). *Beyond GDP: Measuring welfare and assessing sustainability*. Oxford: Oxford University Press.

Frederickson, B. L. (2001). The role of positive emotions in positive psychology: The broaden-and-build theory of positive emotions. *American Psychologist, 56*(3), 218–226.

Freedom House. *Freedom in the world*. Annual report.

Frey, B. S., & Stutzer, A. (2005). *Beyond outcomes: Measuring procedural utility*. Oxford: Economic Papers.

Friedman, M. (1962). *Capitalism and freedom*. Chicago, IL: University of Chicago Press.

Frijda, N. (1988). *De emoties; een overzicht van onderzoek en theorie [The emotions; a review of research and theory]*. Amsterdam: Bert Bakker.

Gerring, J., & Thomas, C. W. (2011). Quantitative and Qualitative: A Question of Comparability. In B. Badie, D. Berg-Schlosser, & L. Morlino (Eds.), *Extended version of chapter published in international encyclopedia of political science*. Thousand Oaks, CA: Sage.

Gilbert, D. (2007). *Stumbling on happiness*. New York: Vintage Books, Random House.

Glatzer, W., Camfield, L., Moller, V., & Rojas, M. (Eds.). *The global handbook of quality of life: Explorations of well-being in nations and continents* (pp. 207–238). Dordrecht: Springer Publishers.

Graham, C. (2017). *Happiness for all?* Princeton, NJ: Princeton University Press.

Griffin, J. (1979). Is unhappiness morally more important than happiness? *The Philosophical Quarterly, 29*(114), 47–55. Oxford University Press, on behalf of the Scots Philosophical Association and the University of St. Andrews.

Griffin, J. (1986). *Well-being: Its meaning, measurement, and moral importance*. Oxford: Clarendon.

Guven, C. (2011). Are happier people better citizens? *Kyklos, 64*(2), 178–192.

Gwartney, J., Lawson, R., & Hall, J. (2017). *Economic freedom of the world: 2017 annual report*. Vancouver: Fraser Institute.

Hayek, F. (1944). *The road to serfdom*. London: Routledge Press, University of Chicago Press.

Headey, B., & Wearing, A. (1992). *Understanding happiness: A theory of subjective well-being*. Melbourne: Longman Cheshire Pty Limited.

Helliwell, J. (2018). Empirical linkages between good governance and national well-being. *Journal of Comparative Economics*. https://doi.org/10.1016/j.jce.2018.01.004.

Helliwell, J. F., Layard, R., Sachs, J., & De Neve, J.-E. (Eds.). (2020). *World happiness report 2020*. New York: Sustainable Development Solutions Network.

Helliwell, J., & Huang, H. (2008). How is your government? International evidence linking good government and well-being. *The British Journal of Political Science, 38*, 595–619.

Helliwell, J., Layard, R., & Sachs, J. (2012, 2017, 2018). *World happiness report 2012, 2017, 2018*. World Happiness Report 2012: Chapter 2: The State of World Happiness; Comparing Different Measures. New York: Sustainable Development Solutions Network.

Hirata, J. (2001). *Happiness and economics: Enriching economic theory with empirical psychology*. Master's thesis, Maastricht University.

Hirata, J. (2011). *Happiness, ethics and economics*. London and New York: Routledge, Taylor & Francis Group.

Hochrat, O., & Skopek, N. (2013). The impact of wealth on subjective well-being: A comparison of three welfare-state regimes. *Research in Social Stratification and Mobility, 34*, 127–141.

Hume, D. (1751). *Enquiry concerning the principles of morals*.

Hutcheson, F. (1725). *Inquiry concerning moral good and evil*.

Hyman, L. (2014). *Happiness: Understandings, narratives and discourses*. Basingstoke: Palgrave Macmillan.

Jans-Beken, L. (2018). *Appreciating gratitude, new perspectives on the gratitude-mental health connection*. Heerlen: Open University.

Kahneman, D. (1999). Objective happiness. In D. Kahneman, E. Diener, & N. Schwartz (Eds.), *Well-being: The foundation of hedonic psychology* (pp. 3–25). New York: Russell Sage Foundation.

Kahneman, D., Kreuger, A. B., & Schkade, D. A. (2004). A survey method for characterizing daily life experience: The day reconstruction method. *Science, 306*, 1776–1780.

Kainulainen, S., & Veenhoven, R. (2018). Life-satisfaction is more a matter of feeling-well than having -what-you-want. *International Journal of Happiness and Development, 4*(3), 209–235.

Kant, I. (1795). *Groundwork of the metaphysics of morals*.

Kapteyn, A., et al. (2015). Dimensions of subjective well-being. *Social Indicators Research, 123*(3), 625–660.

Kaufmann, D. (2005). Back to basics, 10 myths about governance and corruption. *Finance and Development, 42*(3), 41–43. (Myth 4).

Kaufmann, D., Kraay, A., & Mastruzzi, M. (2010). *The worldwide governance indicators: Methodology and analytical issues*. In the World Bank Policy Research Working Paper No. 5430.

Keyes, C. L. (2005). Mental illness and/or mental health? Investigating axioms of the complete state model of health. *Journal of Clinical Psychology, 73*(3), 539–548.

Kiley Hamlin, J., et al. (2013). Not like me = bad: Infants prefer those who harm dissimilar others. *Psychological Science, 24*(4), 589–594.

Knight, F. H. (1964). *Risk, uncertainty, and profit*. New York: A.M. Kelly.

Kraut, R. (2007). *What is good and why*. Cambridge, MA and London: Harvard University Press.

Kuznets, S. (1955). Toward a theory of economic growth. In R. Lekachman (Ed.), *National policy for economic welfare at home and abroad*. Garden City, NY: Doubleday & Co.

Lane, R. (2000). *The loss of happiness in market democracies*. New Haven & London: Yale University Press.

Layard, R. (1980). Human satisfaction and public policy. *The Economic Journal, 90*(360), 737–750.

Layard, R. (2011). *Happiness, lessons from a new science* (2nd ed.). London and New York: Penguin.

Layard, R. (2018). Mental illness destroys happiness and is costless to treat. In J. Sachs (Ed.), *Global happiness: Policy report 2018* (pp. 27–52). New York: Sustainable Development Solutions Network.

Lefcowits, M. J., & Wallston, B. (1973). Self-anchoring scale: Does it make a difference? *Sociological Methods & Research, 1*(3), 387–399. Sage Publications.

Lichtenberg, J. (1996). Consuming because others consume. *Social Theory & Practice, 22*(3), 273–297.

Lucas, R., Clark, A. E., Georgellis, Y., & Diener, E. (2004). Unemployment alters the set-point for life satisfaction. *Psychological Science, 15*(1), 8–13.

Mandeville B. (1714–1729). The fable of the bees, private vices, public benefits.

Maslow, A. H. (1943). A theory of human motivation. *Psychological Review, 50*(4), 370–396.

Mazzucato, M., & Skidelsky, R. (2020). *Toward a new fiscal constitution*. Project Syndicate. Retrieved from https://www.project-syndicate.org/.

McMahon, D. (2005). *Happiness, a history*. New York: Atlantic Monthly Press.

McMahon, F. (2012). Human freedom from Pericles to measurement. *The Independent Review: A Journal of Political Economy, 19*(1), 65–84.

Merleau-Ponty, M. (1945). *Phénoménologie de la perception*. Paris: Gallimard.

Michels, R. (1911). *A sociological study of the oligarchical tendencies of modern democracy*. New York: The Free Press.

Mill, J., & Bentham, J. (1987). *Utilitarianism and other essays*. London and New York: Penguin Classics.

Nozick, R. (1974). *Anarchy, state, and utopia* (p. 41).

Nussbaum, A. (2000). *Women and development*. Cambridge: Cambridge University Press.

Ott, J. (2006). Do not trust your own wants if you want to be happy! *Journal of Happiness Studies, 7*(4), 517–522; Review of the book Happiness; the science behind your smile (2005) by Daniel Nettle, UK; Oxford University Press.

Ott, J. (2010). Good governance and happiness in nations: Technical quality precedes democracy and quality beats size. *Journal of Happiness Studies, 11*(3), 353–368.

Ott, J. (2011a). How much competition do we need in a civilized society? *Journal of Happiness Studies, 12*(3), 525–529. Review of Winning: Reflections on an American Obsession (2011) by Francesco Duina; Princeton and Oxford. University Press.

Ott, J. (2011b). Limited experienced happiness or unlimited expected utility, what about the differences? *Journal of Happiness Studies, 12*(3), 519–524. (Review of the book Happiness around the world: The paradox of happy peasant and miserable millionaires (2009) by Carol Graham; New York, NY: Oxford University Press.

Ott, J. (2013). Science and morality: Mind the gap, use happiness as a safe bridge! *Journal of Happiness Studies, 14*(1), 345–351.

Ott, J. (2015). Impact of size and quality of governments on happiness: Financial insecurity as a key-problem in market-democracies. *Journal of Happiness Studies, 16*(6), 1639–1647.

Ott, J. (2018). Measuring economic freedom, better without size of government. *Social Indicators research, 135*(2), 479–498.

Ott, J., & McMahon, F. (2018). Is freedom just about the absence of inhibitions, or also about the availability of options? Published on line in *Social Indicators Research.* https://doi.org/10.1007/s11205-018-1897-0.

Pavot, W., & Diener, E. (2013). Positive and negative affect are experienced relatively independent of each other. In S. David, I. Boniwell, & A. C. Ayers (Eds.), *Chapter 10 of the oxford handbook of happiness.*

Philips, J., et al. (2017). True happiness: The role of morality in the folk concept of happiness. *Journal of Experimental Psychology, 146*(2), 165–181.

Piketty, T. (2013). *Capital in the twenty-first century.* Cambridge, MA: Éditions du Seuil; Harvard University Press.

Popper, K. (1945). *The open society and its enemies.* (p. 548). London and New York: Routledge Classics.

Rawls, J. (1999). *A theory of justice* (revised ed.). Cambridge, MA: Harvard University Press.

Rice, C. (2013). Defending the objective list theory of well-being. *Ratio, An International Journal of Analytic Philosophy, 26*(2), 196–211. Wiley & Sons Ltd.

Rodriguez-Pose, A., & Maslauskaite, K. (2011). Can policy make us happier? Individual characteristics, socio-economic factors and life satisfaction in Central and Eastern Europe. *Cambridge Journal of Regions, Economy and Society, 2011*, 1–20.

Rothstein, B., & Uslaner, E. M. (2005). All for all: Equality, corruption, and social trust. *World Politics, 58*(1), 41–72.

Ryle, G. (1949). *The concept of mind*. Chicago, IL: University of Chicago Press. (edition 2002).

Samuel, R., & Hadjar, A. (2016). How welfare-state regimes shape subjective well-being across Europe. *Social Indicators Research, 129*, 565–587.

Schkade, D. A., & Kahneman, D. (1998). Does living in California make people happy? A focusing illusion in judgements of life satisfaction. *Psychological Science, 9*, 340–346. Network. (9th report, first report in 2012).

Sen, A. (1985). *Commodities and capabilities*. Professor Dr. P. Hennipman Lectures in Economics. Amsterdam, North Holland.

Sen, A. (1999a). *Development as freedom*. New York: Anchor Books, Random House.

Sen, A. (1999b). *Capabilities and commodities*. Oxford: Oxford University Press.

Sen, A. (2010). *The idea of justice*. London: Penguin books.

Smith, A. (1776). *The wealth of nations*.

Smith, A. (First version in 1759; last version in 1790). *Theory of moral sentiments*. Mineola, NY: Dover Publications, Inc.

Stiglitz, J. (2012). *The price of inequality*. New York: W.W. Norton & Company.

Sumner, L. W. (1996). *Welfare, Happiness, And Ethics*. New York: Oxford University Press.

Taylor, T. (2012). *Knowing what is good for you*. Basingstoke: Palgrave Macmillan.

Tönnies, F. (1887). *Gemeinschaft und Gesellschaft*.

Tversky, A., & Griffin, D. (1991). Endowment and contrast in judgements of well-being. In F. Strack, M. Argyle, & N. Schwartz (Eds.), *Subjective well-being: An interdisciplinary perspective* (pp. 101–118). Oxford: Pergamon.

Van Praag, B., & Ferrer-i-Carbonell, A. (2004). *Happiness quantified. A satisfaction calculus approach*. Oxford: Oxford University Press.

Veenhoven, R. (1984). *Conditions of happiness*. Dordrecht: Kluwer Academic Publishers.

Veenhoven, R. (2008a). Comparability of happiness across nations. *School of Sociology and Social Work Journal, 104*, 211–234.

Veenhoven, R. (2008b, June 21–22). *Freedom and happiness: Comparison of 126 nations in 2006*. Paper presented at Legatum prosperity workshop, London.

Veenhoven, R. (2009). *How do we assess how happy we are?* Tenets, implications and tenability of three theories'. In A. K. Dutt & B. Radcliff (Eds.), *Happiness, economics and politics: Towards a multi-disciplinary approach*. Cheltenham: Edward Elgar Publishers, Chapter 3, pp. 45–69.

Veenhoven, R. (2017). Measures of happiness: Which to choose? In G. Brulé & F. Maggino (Eds.), *Metrics of well-being, Part II measurement issues* (pp. 65–84). Dordrecht: Springer.

Veenhoven, R. *World database of happiness*. Rotterdam: Erasmus University Rotterdam. Retrieved from http://worlddatabaseofhappiness.eur.nl.

Vendrik, M., & Hirata, J. (2003). Experienced versus decision utility of income: Relative or absolute happiness. In L. Bruni & P. L. Porta (Eds.), *Handbook of the economics of happiness* (pp. 185–208). Cheltenham: Edward Elgar.

Watson, D., Clark, L., & Tellegen, A. (1988). Development and validation of brief measures of positive and negative affect: The PANAS scales. *Journal of Personality and Social Psychology, 54*, 1063–1070.

Weber, M. (1919). *Wissenschaft als Beruf (1917–1919) und Politik als Beruf.*

Wentholt, R. (1980). *Motivation theory.* Unpublished reader. Erasmus University Rotterdam, Rotterdam.

Wilkinson, R. (2005). *The impact of inequality: How to make sick societies healthier.* London: Routledge.

Wolff, E. (2010, March). *Recent trends in household wealth in the United States: Rising debt and the middle-class squeeze- an update to 2007.* Levy Institute, Working paper no. 589.

Zajonc, R. (1984). On the primacy of affect. *American Psychologist, 39*(2), 117–123.

# Index[1]



[1] Note: Page numbers followed by 'n' refer to notes.


J. Ott, *Beyond Economics*,
https://doi.org/10.1007/978-3-030-56600-5

## G



## H

## L



## M



## N



## O

The manufacturer's authorised representative in the EU is Springer Nature Customer Service Centre GmbH, Europaplatz 3, 69115 Heidelberg, Germany. If you have any concerns regarding our products, please contact ProductSafety@springernature.com

Printed and bound by CPI Group (UK) Ltd, Croydon, CR0 4YY

22/09/2026

02221061-0004